# experience THE blessing

GENERAL EDITOR
# JOHN ARNOTT

**Renew**
FROM REGAL

**A Division of Gospel Light**
Ventura, California, U.S.A.

Published by Renew Books
A Division of Gospel Light
Ventura, California, U.S.A.
Printed in the U.S.A.

Renew Books is a ministry of Gospel Light, an evangelical Christian publisher dedicated to serving the local church. We believe God's vision for Gospel Light is to provide church leaders with biblical, user-friendly materials that will help them evangelize, disciple and minister to children, youth and families.

It is our prayer that this Renew book will help you discover biblical truth for your own life and help you meet the needs of others. May God richly bless you.

*For a free catalog of resources from Renew Books/Gospel Light, please call your Christian supplier or contact us at* 1-800-4-GOSPEL *or* www.gospellight.com.

Cover and interior design by Robert Williams
Edited by Deena Davis and Evelyn Pedersen

LIBRARY OF CONGRESS CATALOGING-IN-PUBLICATION DATA
Experience the Blessing / John Arnott, general editor
    p. cm.
  Includes bibliographical references
  ISBN 0-8307-2766-3 (pbk.)
    1. Toronto blessing. I. Arnott, John (John G.)
  BR1644.7 C74 2001
  269'.2—dc21
                                  00-045692

1 2 3 4 5 6 7 8 9 10 11 12 13 14 15 / 09 08 07 06 05 04 03 02 01 00

Rights for publishing this book in other languages are contracted by Gospel Literature International (GLINT). GLINT also provides technical help for the adaptation, translation and publishing of Bible study resources and books in scores of languages worldwide. For further information, contact GLINT, P.O. Box 4060, Ontario, CA 91761-1003, U.S.A. You may also send e-mail to Glintint@aol.com, or visit their website at www.glint.org.

# contents

# foreword

What the witnesses in this book report of their encounter with the manifest presence of God will be familiar to practically anyone who has attended meetings in recent years at the Toronto Airport Christian Fellowship. The Toronto phenomenon is not conceptual and does not lie in points of doctrine. This explains why it is so inclusive of believers from every tradition and culture. It explains how a Catholic priest can give a testimony and receive a huge round of applause and how a Baptist (like me) can mix with Anglicans and Presbyterians and Pentecostals without a second thought. This is not a new theology; it is an old theology caught on fire.

The essential contribution of the Toronto Blessing lies in its spirituality of playful celebration. The Day of Pentecost (let us not forget) was a festival in the Jewish calendar, and its festive character is evident in the Toronto meetings—in the joy and laughter of God's children playing in the presence of God. When the music sounds, the people burst into joyful praise and abandon themselves to the love of God being poured out.

Different images are used of this abandon to the Holy Spirit's presence—catch the fire, enter the river, come to the party, soak in the Spirit—because there is much to be experienced. The preaching may be poor (although this is not common) and the distractions may be many (you get used to them), but one thing you can count on is the felt presence of God. It seems as if God has pitched his tent on Attwell Drive so that when you enter the place, expectancy rises and anticipation builds. The people come wanting more of God and certain that God will move. They come wanting to be filled with God's fullness. And they cry, "More, Lord! More of you!" which is a prayer God loves to hear.

I have a picture in my mind about this gathering. I see an ocean of happy faces, a swirl of colorful flags, an outbreak of dancing. I hear robust singing and mysterious stillness, and always there is dynamism and spontaneity. When thousands are present, there is still the participation of everyone. And when there are only hundreds, you still taste the kindness of the Lord. People meet God there in ways that contrast remarkably with the poverty of feeling and the fear of the Body so prevalent in some established churches, from which so many have come like thirsty refugees. Nowadays "play" is reserved for the sports field. The fun has gone out of religion, making it boring and rigid. The Toronto Blessing says this does not have to be. Christianity can be alive and energizing.

What do the people come to celebrate? Not raw experience or contentless mysticism, but the Father's love. They want to grasp, as the apostle Paul urges us, how broad and long and high and deep is the love that surpasses knowledge; and they want it to roll over them like ocean waves. It is not enough to express belief in it—knowing about it is not enough. Doctrine is no substitute for a love affair. In Toronto, the Bride of Christ wants to fall in love with Jesus again. This relationship of love is not just an aspect of our faith, it is its centerpiece. The apostle John says, "God is love" (1 John 4:8), essentially and fundamentally; and at the heart of the Toronto Blessing is the celebration of that relationship. Here, people receive God's love and give love back in response. Here, God reaches out and people respond with the kind of enthusiasm that God longs for. We celebrate a relationship that is not manipulative or legalistically slavish; it is mutual, interactive and transforming.

The worship in Toronto is the ancient liturgy of the Church revitalized, with its many parts present but unnamed: the call, the gloria, the kyrie, the confession, the Word and the benediction. The old structures are there and are now carried along by an oral tradition that allows for both form and freedom. As is characteristic of jazz music, themes are pronounced by leaders but are also enriched by improvisation coming from the people and fueled by testimonies of what the Lord has done. The Scriptures are expounded, not literalistically, but charismatically, such that the Word of the Lord sounds fresh from the ancient texts. In a playful interaction between what the Bible presents and the present situation, the story line of Scripture gets interwoven with the life of the community so that we recognize ourelves in the text and are challenged by the living Word.

In traditional worship, God's truth comes across through word and sacrament but often at the expense of participation. People are limited to singing hymns and repeating fixed responses, which makes worship static and pretty uneventful. But in Toronto there is room for dynamic and spontaneous responses. People freely react to what is going on with approval, applause, laughter and lament. In doing so, the Western bias against the intuitive and the physical is also partly overcome. Space is given to reports of dreams and visions—a realm in which we experience reality of a different order—and permission is given to experience bodily reactions, physical sensations and prayers for the healing of the broken creation. These features, which others may put down to emotionalism and excess, are not often restrained because there is no desire to confine God to a box—better the chaos of celebration than the peaceful order of a cemetery.

Something has been discovered here that has often gone missing in other churches. Theology has typically concentrated on two dimensions of Christian experience—justification and sanctification—but has said little about a third element: baptism in the Holy Spirit. Many churches have also ignored this third element, perhaps because it frightens them. Yet it was this baptism that the disciples needed before they could go forward in mission. They were told to wait for it, and they prayed for God to give them His presence to empower them so that they could give effective expression to His reality. Through the Toronto Blessing and other such movements today, God is challenging the Church, not to quench the Holy Spirit, but to earnestly desire the power of God.

Jesus was a singer and God's troubadour. Once He said, "We played the flute for you, and you did not dance" (Matt 11:17). The Lord is still saying that. When you hear the music, won't you respond? Won't you overcome the dualisms of body versus spirit and of mind versus heart? Can't you leave your left-brained Christianity behind? The testimonies in this book declare that the table is set and the wine is flowing. The words invite everyone everywhere to come to the banquet of God!

—Clark H. Pinnock

*Dr. Clark H. Pinnock has taught at the University of Manchester in England, New Orleans Baptist Theological Seminary, Trinity Evangelical Divinity School near Chicago, Regent College in Vancouver, and since 1977, McMaster Divinity College in Ontario. He is the author of a number of books, including* Flame of Love *and* A Wideness in God's Mercy.

# Introduction

## THE FATHER'S BLESSING

In many ways, January 20, 1994, seems like so long ago. So much has happened since then in our church, our ministry and our personal lives. Carol and I felt that we were the least qualified to lead a revival that would eventually have worldwide impact, yet we had to stop asking "Why me?" and embrace what God was asking of us.

Like Mary of old, we also had to say to Him, "Be it done unto me according to Thy word" (Luke 1:38, *KJV*). A dear friend pointed out to us that Mary was asked to do something much greater than what we were being asked—she was asked to be the mother of the Messiah and raise Him to the place where He would take up His ministry as the Son of God and Savior of the world. Our assignment was small by comparison. So Carol and I said yes and then ran with it.

You need to know that the fresh and powerful experiences of the Holy Spirit that you will read about in the following pages are also intended for you. Yet so many have stumbled over the fact that the experiences are powerful and the manifestations are way beyond anything most of us have ever seen before. Carol and I are constantly redirecting the attention of people away from the look of the manifestations and onto the fruit in the person's life. At one level I like to ask, "Why are we surprised that a touch from God is powerful?" If God really touches us, even a little, the miracle is that we live to tell the story!

My friend Dr. Ralph Neighbour points out that there are three ways of learning: cognitive, psychomotor and affective. Cognitive learning takes place when we have a textbook and a teacher and we use our reasoning and memorization skills to download information into our heads that results in understanding. Cognitive learning is, of course, very needful, even when learning about the things of God and His Word; but it is not the only means of gaining understanding.

Psychomotor learning involves the motor skills and responses of the body. We practice with the aid of an instructor until we become proficient in skills like skiing, golf, playing the piano or public speaking. This also is a very important learning process.

Affective learning takes place when we have an experience that affects us—that makes an impact on our bodies and emotions as well as our minds, and the experience often needs to be explained. These kinds of experiences can have a powerful effect on the whole person and can leave us wondering, *What happened?* An experience changes our values for better or for worse. An experience with God will be life changing, as it was for Saul of Tarsus. He was thrown to the ground and blinded, but he was changed forever.

Consider Ephesians 3:19 *(NKJV):* "to know the love of Christ which passes knowledge; that you may be filled with all the fullness of God." There is a place deep in the heart of each person that hungers for a profound and moving encounter with the person of God—a meeting that reaches deep into the innermost being and satisfies the inner longings of the heart. Can we be like those in the Bible who had a divine encounter with the Holy Spirit? Those God seekers became world changers!

Carol and I have shared many hundreds of times with leaders and pastors, responding to their frequently asked questions: Why you? Who are you, anyway? What did you do to help bring this about? How has this impacted your life personally? How has your ministry changed? Have you and Carol been touched by these powerful manifestations of the Holy Spirit? Why is this surrounded by so much controversy? How can I be sure I don't get a counterfeit? Where do you think it is all going? How can this revival come to my church?

Our testimony is a common enough story. We grew increasingly tired during the '80s, attempting to see our church people healed up and set free from sin and problems. There was always one more hurt to be healed and one more demon to deal with. When we went to Benny Hinn's crusade in Toronto late in the summer of 1992, we realized in a fresh, new way that it was the power of the Holy Spirit that was missing in our lives and ministries. We had to have more. We decided to give our mornings to the Lord in prayer, Bible reading and worship. It changed our lives. We fell back in love with Jesus during this precious season in our lives.

The defining moment came when we went to Argentina with Ed Silvoso. We went along to witness the revival happening in that nation. We saw the Almos prison—an institution transformed by the power of God. We attended a powerful crusade with Carlos Anacondia. Then, Claudio Freidzon prayed for us, and our lives were permanently changed. My wife, Carol, was completely overwhelmed by the Holy Spirit's power upon her. She was laughing, rolling and could not walk straight. I was aware of an impartation of faith for more of God and for miracles. It seems so obvious in hindsight, but at the time it left me wondering what—if anything—had changed.

We came home with heightened expectations and were excited to learn that Randy Clark, pastor of the St. Louis Vineyard, had been on a similar pilgrimage and was mightily touched at a Rodney Howard-Browne meeting. We invited him to come to Toronto for four days of meetings. The first night, January 20, 1994, Randy gave his testimony and invited our church people to come up for prayer. The Holy Spirit fell on us, and that was the beginning. We have subsequently been wonderfully touched many times. Our lives have been changed forever. Our church of 360 is now 10 times larger and still seeing rapid growth. And best of all, a transferable revival anointing has spread around the world.

So why the controversy? It just seems to always go along with revival. It was true in Jonathan Edwards's day, and it is true in our day. In it all, I think God is very interested in discerning the motivation of the heart. Do you really love Him, or are you merely after successful ministry? Is it Him you desire, or do you merely want to be bailed out of life's problems? I have learned one thing: If you come as a little child, asking your heavenly Father for bread, He will not give you a stone (see Luke 11:11). When we, in childlike faith, ask our loving Father for more of the Holy Spirit, He will not disappoint us. Carol and I feel that this is best summed up in the words of Sarah Edwards, wife of Jonathan Edwards, as she attempted to explain why she was so overcome for 19 consecutive days during the Great Awakening. "I am overwhelmed with His nearness to me and my dearness to Him."

Hear now the testimonies of Christian leaders as they share from their hearts some of the deep things God has done in their lives along with the long-term fruit. In the following pages, you are going to meet a medical doctor whose career took on a whole new dimension after an encounter with the Holy Spirit. You will read about a dynamic missionary couple who received fresh strength for their ministry among Mozambique's orphans. God has now given them the nation! You will read about a television producer whose skepticism was overcome by seeing the grace of God at work in his daughter; a scholar whose theology on the Holy Spirit was revolutionized; a well-known worship leader whose worship style radically altered; and a sociologist who found out that being touched by the Holy Spirit produces amazingly good fruit in a person's life.

Are you tired of fruitless ministry? Are you hungry and thirsty for more of God's Holy Spirit? Jesus says, "If anyone thirsts, let him come to Me and drink. *He who believes in Me, as the Scripture has said, out of his heart will flow rivers of living water*" (John 7:37,38, *NKJV*, emphasis added). With an open heart, listen to the stories of these prominent leaders who came to the Lord hungry, even desperate, and in other cases, skeptical. Now they can testify that they have received exceeding abundantly above all they could ask or think.

—John Arnott

# running life's race

## SCOTT McDERMOTT

*Scott McDermott is senior pastor of Washington Crossing United Methodist Church, in Pennsylvania and holds a doctorate in New Testament studies from Drew University. He is an adjunct professor at Southern Methodist University. He was invited to a meeting in Florida, hosted by the Charismatic Concerns Committee. I was also invited to come and share about what was happening with the revival in Toronto. We prayed for Scott, and he had one of the most incredible encounters with God that I have ever witnessed. Here is his story. —J. A.*

In the spring of 1996, I received an invitation to attend a meeting in Orlando, Florida. The invitation was to attend a discussion group of Christian leaders—people concerned with renewal of the Church, mediating differences, and promoting unity and understanding in the Body of Christ. My first inclination was to stay home, but something within me said I should attend.

During this same time, I had been mulling over many questions about the work of the Holy Spirit. I wondered about Toronto. Could it be true that God was really at work there? What about all those unusual manifestations? Were they really from God, or were they the product of an overactive imagination? As I reviewed the list of presenters at the discussion conference in Orlando, I was struck with the fact that John Arnott would be there to discuss the Father's Blessing, as well as the controversy surrounding the events occurring at his church, the Toronto Airport Christian Fellowship. *Curious,* I thought.

*Here I am with these questions about Toronto, and right before me stands the perfect opportunity to have some of them answered.*

I was not a newcomer to the topic of renewal. The charismatic renewal had touched my life deeply in the early '70s. Nor was I new to the present wind of the Spirit that began to blow on the Church in 1994. Our own congregation, Washington Crossing United Methodist Church, had received a merciful and surprising touch of the Spirit in the same year, leading us into a series of protracted meetings, long hours of prayer and, yes, even people doing "carpet time" on our sanctuary floor. But that was our congregation—with people I knew and with expressions of the Spirit I had seen before.

What I heard about Toronto just seemed too extreme, too emotional and too over the edge for my liking. But since the Father's Blessing was being talked about at every turn, I felt the least I could do was give John Arnott a fair hearing. Then when my own parishioners asked me about it, I would be able to speak more intelligently about what was transpiring in Toronto. So I set out for Florida to get my questions answered.

John Arnott was hardly what I had expected. He was far from the emotional "work you up into a frenzy" kind of man I would have associated with such a movement. Instead, he was gentle, soft-spoken and humble as he presented an overview of the events that had transpired in his church since January 1994. He anchored his sharing in Ezekiel 47, a passage that describes the renewing work that takes place through the river of God. He also provided a recent report by sociologist Dr. Margaret Poloma, who detailed the life changes that took place for many after receiving prayer in Toronto.

While John's presentation was quite helpful, I still had some questions about the manifestations associated with this work of the Spirit. Since the meeting of leaders was small and informal,

I was able to ask John about this controversial aspect of his ministry. His response was not defensive. Instead, he made it clear that these physical responses to the Spirit were not his focus, nor was he encouraging these responses. He was more concerned with the changes that took place in a person's life than with the appearance of his or her encounter with God. It was a reasonable response. After all, as a United Methodist, I couldn't help but think of the way in which John Wesley, the founder of Methodism, responded when people began falling to the ground during his meetings. Rather than condemn it, he sought to understand what was happening by listening carefully to the individuals' experiences (Wesley's journal, June 15, 1739).

# toronto-style prayer

Later that night we gathered for a time of worship and teaching followed by a season of prayer ministry. John was to lead both the teaching and the ministry times. Shortly after 9:00 P.M., the time had come to receive prayer from John. No music was playing, and the harsh fluorescent lights hardly provided a rich and receptive atmosphere for prayer. Yet one by one, people began to fall under the power of the Spirit as John prayed. I was standing near the back of the room, waiting to receive from God but also thinking, *Falling over is just not my thing.* Still, I stood receptive.

When John came to me, nothing happened at first. He began to pray, "More, Lord. More of the Lord." Nothing happened, and I was actually quite okay with that. John then began to pray for the person standing next to me. That person fell over, but I just closed my eyes and said to the Lord, "I'm not going to look around; I'm just going to focus on You, Lord." Just then, John stepped back to pray for me. To my amazement I soon found myself on the floor! As I extended my hands heavenward, my arms began to tremble slightly. At first I wondered why my arms were trembling, but my attention was soon drawn to the fire dancing upon my eyelids. Quickly my mind referenced the biblical passages on fire to better comprehend the significance of what I was experiencing.

John, however, had now moved on to pray for others. At times he would pause in the room and offer a prayer over the whole group. This was one of those moments. John lifted his voice in prayer and said, "Let the fire of the Spirit come in this room." Trembling and still aware of the flames, I heard the Lord say to me, "You be the oil and I'll be the fire." No sooner had I heard this than I began to feel gentle, pulsating waves of the Spirit move over my body. One gentle wave after another came, delicately and slowly flowing from the top of my head to my feet and then back again. From somewhere in the room, John lifted his voice and prayed again, "We welcome the wave of the Spirit here in this room. Let the waves of the Spirit just come. One wave after another."

The next thing I knew I was standing in the brown and desolate Judean wilderness, not far from the city of Jericho. In front of me stood a large and deep canyon that was a part of the Wadi Qelt. As I looked across the wadi, my eyes began to focus on an area of contrasting green vegetation that flourished on the canyon wall. There in the middle of all the green, I saw a steady stream of water gushing out of the hillside into the canyon below. As I stood transfixed by this refreshing and compelling contrast, the Lord said to me, "I want you to be living water to the people I have given you to pastor. Be like fresh water to them." No sooner did I hear this than John, still ministering to people in other parts of the room, prayed over us again: "Let the living water well up within your belly. Let the water of the Holy Spirit just well up within you."

The scene changed and I found myself running on the road that leads from Jericho to Jerusalem. This road runs 18 miles along a winding and mountainous terrain, ascending nearly 3,300 feet as it makes its way from the Jordan Valley to the heights of Jerusalem. At times the roadway skirts the edge of the adjacent canyon, while at other times it slowly curls through the Judean hillside. Despite the hills and the difficulty of the road, the run was easy. Even when the hills seemed steep and difficult, it felt as if I were running downhill or as if the roadway itself were pushing me along.

I began to cry for the sheer wonder of what I was experiencing. I asked the Lord, "Why is this so easy?" He replied, "Your heart is set on Jerusalem, and when your heart is set on Jerusalem the hills are light."

As I lay there on the floor, I became aware that my legs and arms were moving as if I were actually running. Every now and then, as I ran along the road, a person or two appeared on the roadside, clapping for me as I passed. The Lord began to speak to me a combination of verses from the books of Joshua and 1 Corinthians. He exhorted me, "Don't you turn to the left or the right. Run the race that is set before you, but don't run aimlessly. Run the race; run to win the prize." Those words resonated with the deep longings of my heart. I knew I had to run to win. So run I did! I began to open up my stride, and my breathing began to deepen as I endeavored to pick up the pace.

I didn't realize it until later, but apparently my actions were not going unnoticed. Indeed, the concern of others had grown so great that at least one person wanted to stop what was happening to me. John Arnott, however, thought better of it and suggested that first they must discern what was happening to me. (This response can serve as a model for all of us when we encounter things we at first do not understand.)

John walked over to me, bent down and said, "Scott, what is God doing?" I explained to him, "I'm running the road from Jericho to Jerusalem." Then I added, "I'm running uphill, but it feels like I'm running downhill." John repeated my words to the others. With a quivering voice and tears gently streaming down my face, I told him that the Lord said the road was easy because my heart was set on Jerusalem. John once again repeated my message to onlookers and then said, "He's having a vision."

I'll never forget what happened next. I was still running the road from Jericho to Jerusalem when John placed his hand on my chest and began to pray, "Go for it, Scott! Go for it! Win the race, Scott! Go for it! Run to Jerusalem! More, Lord! More, Lord! More, Lord!" The more John prayed, the more I wanted to run. A new resolve began to emerge in my heart. My breathing intensified with each step toward the goal. As I ran, more people gathered along the roadside, clapping and cheering.

Just as I was wondering when this was going to end, I found myself in the village of Bethany. A great crowd had gathered on each side of the roadway that went to the top of the Mount of Olives. The people were shouting my name and cheering me on. I ran through the village and up the steep grade of the Mount of Olives as if I were running the 100-yard dash. Now in full stride, I went over the top of the Mount, down the precipitous slope, and through the garden of Gethsemane and the Kidron Valley toward the Eastern Gate of the Temple mount.

As I approached, I could see that the once walled and sealed city gate was now open. Stretched across the opening was a finish line. And there, on the other side, stood Jesus with arms outstretched and beckoning, a smile of delight radiating from His face. I collapsed across the finish line into my Savior's loving arms. Jesus held me ever so tightly, laughing with delight while I wept in His arms. All around Him stood the faithful servants—those who had run the race before me. These servants were also laughing in delight. I could feel their pats on my back as they said, "Did you feel our prayers? We have been praying for your every step!"

The race was over, but my moment with Jesus was not. He indicated the people around Him and said to me, "You go with them." *Go with them*? I thought. *I do not belong with them. After all, these are His faithful servants! Surely He must be wrong.* Feelings of unworthiness filled my being as I sobbed before Him, "No! Not me! I don't belong with these people, Lord! These are Your faithful servants!" The more I objected, the more He looked at me with affirmation in His eyes; and He then said, "You go with them. That's where you belong." His love transcended my own unworthiness. With each word and each look, there was an impartation of irresistible and indescribable love. That love filled my entire being until it made even my unworthiness surrender to the bidding of His will.

Having surrendered to His wishes, I found myself now being carried by the faithful witnesses. I was still crying, but they continued to laugh as if to say "You'll get over it." I assumed they meant I would get over the tears, for I am sure we will never cease to marvel at the greatness of His love for us. They carried me until I found myself among a multitude so large that I could not even guess their number.

The place where we assembled looked in some ways like the Temple mount in Jerusalem. It was indescribable in size and beauty. Jesus sat before this large gathering and began to speak. He said, "I want all of My faithful servants to stand." He waved His arm in the direction of this vast army. As the multitude stood, the heavens rang out with songs of praise and adoration!

My sobbing ceased and I was aware that I was in Orlando, in an intimate gathering of prominent Christian teachers and writers. I became even more aware that I had been crying and yelling, even running on the floor! I cannot begin to tell you the embarrassment I felt as this realization hit home. When I got to my feet, I was careful not to make eye contact with anyone; but I found it difficult to walk or, should I say, to walk straight! My Bible and calendar were located opposite the exit. Slowly I made my way across and back, but I found it difficult to line up the doorway for a quick exit. One dear man said to me, "Scott, why don't you sit down here?" So I did, thinking, *I will get a quick breath and get up and leave.*

John had noticed me and now came over to speak to me. "Scott, it seems that God was doing something really interesting in your life. Would you mind sharing it with the group?" *Well,* I thought, *why not? I have already lost every ounce of reputation I might have had before these people; the least I can do is describe what was happening to me.* So I shared what I had been experiencing and just cried before them.

On the flight home, I realized that God had answered my questions about Toronto in a way I had not expected. I went to Florida seeking only an explanation of the events transpiring in Toronto. God chose to give me a personal example.

I looked out the window to the green landscape below, trying to identify the cities and states we were flying over. My eyes, however, were soon drawn to the rivers. They were easy to pick out on such a clear day as they wound their way to the ocean. What struck me was the lush green that seemed to follow their courses. I was reminded again of the words from Ezekiel 47, which tell us that everywhere the river flows there is life. I reflected on the way in which the river of life had touched me so powerfully in Orlando and thought about how I would explain this to Washington Crossing United Methodist Church.

## a surprising reception

At first I told very few people of my experience—only my wife and my closest friends. But within a month I shared it with my staff and in the next few months, with the key leadership of the church. Five months later, in October 1996, I shared with the church what had happened to me. I was not sure what the congregation would say or do once they heard I had been touched by the Father's Blessing. But as I finished sharing that Sunday morning, the congregation stood to their feet and clapped and cheered just like the people in the vision!

One of the most profound differences since my experience with the Holy Spirit has been in my understanding of God's love for me. Although I have never doubted His love, now there is within my heart a deep and constant assurance of it that beckons me along life's pathway to the final heavenly destination. While this concept may seem simple, I would suggest that it is not. I think this knowledge is why Paul continually prayed that the Ephesians would have a revelation of God's boundless love for them. As we travel along the pathway of life—through the twists and turns, precipitous hills and dangerous valleys—we can easily find our comfort and peace threatened.

Along with this indescribable love has come a new resolve to do His will, at any cost. When I went to Orlando in 1996, our church was experiencing a lot of transitions. The changes affected everything—worship, Sunday teaching, small groups, even church infrastructure and decision making. But there comes a time when a pastor has to say in love but with conviction, "Here is where we are going, and we're not going back!" I felt a new resolve to do just that after my encounter with God in Orlando. I now had a race to run and, no matter what it would cost me, I had made the final decision in my heart to finish the race. That resolve continues to this day.

Finally, the Lord has encouraged me greatly. Do you remember my mention of those people in the vision who were clapping and cheering me on? What I didn't tell you was that up until that time in my life, I had found it very difficult to receive words of encouragement from people. I just didn't quite believe them. All of that has changed. Now as people share words that encourage the working of God's grace in my life, I see the people as standing along the roadside, cheering me on to run the race; and I can receive what they have to share with me.

So what about Toronto? Thank God for His glorious outpouring. I want more!

# darkness dispelled

## TED HAGGARD

*We had just been put out of our network of churches when I had to leave Toronto to keep commitments for meetings on the West Coast. There I met Ted Haggard, pastor since 1985 of New Life Church in Colorado Springs and author of several books, including* Primary Purpose: Making It Hard for People to Go to Hell from Your City. *He was very concerned about the pain that the Body of Christ was going through over this split. Ted did his level best to use his influence and expertise to see this rift healed. Unfortunately, it didn't work out, but he has become a true and wonderful friend. Carol and I called him "our angel" during those discouraging weeks. He tells how the Holy Spirit ministered deeply to him in Toronto. —J. A.*

By the mid-1990s, disillusionment was starting to affect every area of my life. I'd seen enough. Apparently dishonest fund-raising, exorbitant salaries, excessively luxurious homes, emotional manipulation, exaggerated testimonies and abuse of spiritual authority had finally gotten to me. I loved the Lord and deeply appreciated the ministry of the Holy Spirit, but I was perplexed by the ethics of our most outspoken representatives of Christ. I found myself snickering and actually agreeing with the cynical bumper stickers that reads "God, please protect me from Your followers!"

On the surface, everything in my life and ministry was going great. My marriage and family life were healthy, the church I was pastoring was growing, and I was being used by the Lord to encourage people. But anger and cynicism were starting to reveal themselves in the most unusual situations. In private with my friends, I found myself making derogatory statements and expressing harsh judgments on the lives of others. I was slowly spiraling downward.

Was I just losing the naïveté of youth, and finally facing the real world, or was I becoming unnecessarily critical of good people? I couldn't determine if I was the problem or if I was surrounded by a church environment that had become more corrupt than the world we were supposed to be serving. The cycles of anger and judgment increased in both depth and frequency, but only my wife and a few close friends noticed—or at least they were the only ones who spoke to me about it.

One morning in the shower, I began to feel like I was dying. I could feel death in my heart; I could hear death whisper into my mind. I knew that the life within me was getting tired. I needed to take action quickly.

I loved the Church, His Bride, too much to have a bitter attitude about her. I concluded that I was the problem, not others. This forced me to examine whether I was simply overworked and approaching burnout or was in midlife crisis. Or could it be that the Lord was working in me in a deeper way, uncovering weak areas in my life? I didn't know exactly why I was feeling the way I was, but I knew that I had to dispel the darkness.

I made arrangements with some of my staff members to go and experience the most powerful services that were drawing the biggest crowds in the country. During a series of trips, we heard great music, listened to dynamic testimonies, heard strong preaching and saw many people being touched. I was often grateful, but at the same time I became increasingly alienated.

I sat through hours of offerings that seemed to me to be spiritually manipulative. I believed many of the things that people were being promised that God would provide for them if they gave. But I resented the setting: lots of big money, big cars and big stadiums. Crowds were flocking to the meetings, driven by the hope that God would touch them. They were stretching their resources to activate His blessing and, sure enough, they were leaving happy and excited. But I couldn't help but question if many of them had only received an emotional touch.

Throughout this process, I avoided Toronto. I'd heard about the falling, twitching, barking, moaning and dancing, with crowds coming from all over the world. And as I listened to the reports, there was a part of me that was revolted. I needed something credible and solid. I needed something that would look like Jesus to me, something that would make me believe that there are humble, genuine and kind leaders who are more concerned for people than for their own security and ministries but who are, at the same time, reaching multitudes. I felt that Toronto would not be my solution but would instead increase my frustration. I was convinced that visiting Toronto would be the last straw that would drive me into spiritual seclusion. I stayed away until there were no more options.

One cold Monday morning in the early spring of 1995, I boarded a plane for Toronto. I was not at all excited to be going, but a visit to this church was my only hope. I needed a miracle and I knew it. Arriving at Pearson International Airport, I found my way to the church in time for the evening meeting. I was immediately shocked: the church was housed in a poorly kept industrial building with crude parking. Nothing was fancy, and everything seemed a little improvised. As I walked in, worship music was playing. The believers who had gathered were unpretentious and *so normal*. Because I was depressed, I didn't want anyone talking to me or making me feel self-conscious. I just wanted to sit by myself and observe.

There were visitors that night from 37 countries. The building was packed, but John and Carol Arnott were not there. A youth pastor from a neighboring church led the meeting, and a senior pastor from yet another local church made the announcements. Everyone on the platform seemed unassuming to me. In fact, if they were evaluated according to professional major-meeting decorum, they were doing a lousy job! Their style was sloppy, slow and too personal.

The offering took place in less than three minutes, with no promises made to the givers. The worship was genuine, and although the preaching was far from profound, it was incredibly compelling. For the first time in my journey through darkness, I didn't feel that the presenters in the front were trying to persuade me. I felt they were just talking to me like a friend in the living room, and I appreciated it.

I knew they couldn't be crooks—crooks were better at religion than this! A part of me wanted to find something wrong, but I couldn't discern anything out of line. I found much that was unorthodox, unusual and unique, but nothing that contradicted Scripture. Certainly there were endless violations of the way major crusades should be run, but nothing that offended my heart. Actually, it was refreshing to see people jam-packed into a simple building with a plain platform, an inadequate sound system and gypsum-rock walls. I relaxed. At the end of the service, I went to stand on one of the lines of red tape adhered to the floor to receive prayer.

As I stood on the line, worshiping and waiting to be prayed for, one of the ministry team members asked me to help him. I spent the next two hours listening to this brother patiently pray for people, and catching those who fell backward. I didn't realize it, but I was, in fact, being soaked in the power of God this whole time. I couldn't focus on myself; I had to focus on others. That was good for me. At the conclusion of the evening (between midnight and 1:00 A.M.) the brother offered to pray for me. I agreed. We prayed quickly and I went back to my hotel room.

The next day I came back for a daytime session. There were not quite so many people there, but this shorter service was very similar in style to the night before. Some people recognized me and welcomed me by name. I didn't mind. I was feeling better. At the end of the meeting, I again went and stood on a red-tape line to receive ministry. As a team member prayed for me, the Holy Spirit began to come upon me. Down I went, and as I lay on the floor, I saw in the Spirit.

There was a round hole in the ceiling. My dad and mom, who had both gone to heaven years ago, were looking down through the hole! They were talking to one another joyfully and smiling at me. I could sense their approval, love and delight at my being able to see them. It was great. They were obviously happy together and thrilled to get a peek at me. We communicated perfectly, but not with words—just by seeing and knowing. There were no unfulfilled desires, no unspoken longings. Instead, it was contentment, deep satisfaction and complete joy. I loved it.

The scene changed, and I saw a meadow similar to the ones in Indiana, where I grew up. I was sitting in the field, very content, but looked up and was thrilled to see the Lord Jesus approaching me! I was neither nervous nor self-conscious; it was just as if I were seeing a wonderful friend. We smiled and greeted one another, and He sat down next to me. In the absence of time we talked and we laughed. There was no hurry, no other commitment, nowhere else to rush off to. We were just there together, Jesus and me.

We spoke of serious things that involved His plan on the earth and in the Church. Then we got up and continued our discussion as we walked throughout the pasture. Our conversation was laced with rabbit trails, side notes, and insights, both serious and funny. It didn't feel at all like a meeting between the awesome God of the universe and lowly created dust: It was like the interaction between two people who thoroughly enjoy one another. It was perfect. It was bliss. It healed me.

While this was happening, I could not tell if I was in my body seeing a vision or out of my body in some other place. But I knew there was no cause for concern and that I was okay. I experienced no fear; and I was free from all thoughts of self, position, intimidation or inadequacy. What I thought of was His perfection, love, light, power, authority and security. His awesome holiness was evident but not intimidating. It never crossed my mind to think of what I was compared to Him, because I enjoyed Him so much. We were one, like a husband and wife so deeply in love that they relish being together, talking and working, or like two friends who are miraculously knit together in heart and soul. That's what it was like to be with Him, and it changed me. And it happened lying on the floor in Toronto.

I returned to my room and thought through the biblical accounts of people who were in the Spirit and saw visions. As I reflected on the experience I had just had, I realized I had been changed. I was no longer in a dark cloud, groping to find my way. Now, five years later, I can report that I've never returned to that awful darkness. Instead, I have an incredible assurance of my place in Christ and my role in His kingdom.

Since that visit in 1995, the church I pastor in Colorado Springs has grown to over 7,000 people. We are woven together through a mysterious anointing, a special presence. It is an unspeakable love that draws, compels and connects us. And I have had a taste of that love because of a meeting I experienced in Toronto, in a church pastored by John and Carol Arnott. I can't tell you how grateful I am to them. They took the risk, opened their hearts and provided a place for people to enter into the Spirit and meet the Master.

# all who are thirsty

## WARREN MARCUS

*Warren Marcus, a messianic Jewish believer ordained in the Baptist church, and an award-winning filmmaker, was brought to our meetings in Toronto by his friend Sid Roth, a well-known radio host and preacher. Not only was Warren spiritually dry, but he was also very skeptical. He had worked in Christian media for many years and had seen it all in terms of gimmicks, hype and emotionalism. Imagine his surprise and delight when his own daughter, whom he had been unsuccessful in winning over to the Lord's plan for her life, was powerfully touched and fell deeply in love with Jesus. —J. A.*

In 1996, messianic Jewish evangelist Sid Roth hired me to produce his new weekly TV program, *It's Supernatural*. The first 13 shows were to be produced in Burlington, Ontario, at the Crossroads studios, home of *100 Huntley Street*. Sid told me that we would be shooting several half-hour programs each day and that each evening he wanted me to go with him to the Toronto Airport Christian Fellowship.

I asked, "Isn't that the place where they bark like dogs?"

Sid laughed and said, "Oh, Warren, that's just what the critics want you to hear. God is moving powerfully. The Spirit of God is so strong there."

I responded, "Sid, I've seen it all. I worked for Pat Robertson's Christian Broadcasting Network for nine years. Every major Spirit-filled minister came there and I've had it with all that stuff. It's just a lot of emotionalism."

Sid objected, but I didn't want to hear it. He finally blurted out, "Well, I'm going to the services. If you want to stay in your hotel room every night, that's your choice. I know I need more from God!"

We went to Canada and Sid was true to his word. Each night, he took everyone in the crew to the church in Toronto. I accompanied him because I didn't want to stay alone in my hotel room. To say I was a skeptic is an understatement. I had heard all the rumors from the critics of this outpouring and believed it was not of God. However, I knew Sid Roth and had trusted his judgment in the past. Still, I felt he may have gone off the deep end on this one.

As we walked into the service that first night, I noticed that people were not in suits and ties—it was very casual. The music was mostly Vineyard, a style with which I was unfamiliar. The worship team members were dressed in jeans and they sounded like a rock band. There were hundreds of people all around me, of every age and ethnic background. Some lifted their hands toward heaven, others bowed, and many were dancing in the aisles and in front by the stage. Some waved flags and banners, while others twirled in circles.

The words of the songs immediately pierced my hardened heart. The lyrics were all so passionate and personal. They were like prayers to God: "I want to know You; I want see Your face." These songs were so refreshing and alive! Conviction filled me as I remembered the relationship I once had with God, when I first became a believer in October 1974.

———

I was born a Jew and grew up in Linden, New Jersey. I was raised in the traditions of the Old Covenant, attended Hebrew School and was bar mitzvahed at the age of 13. Our family attended the synagogue for all the important Jewish holidays, but all the services were in Hebrew. I had been taught to read Hebrew but didn't understand the meaning behind the words. I found my religion to be an empty form, without the power and presence of God. But not one of my Gentile neighbors ever told me about Jesus.

From 1967 through 1970 I attended the School of Visual Arts in New York City to study motion picture production. There I was introduced to drugs. I tried almost everything, including LSD, marijuana, speed and cocaine. I also became involved with radical left-wing politics.

At the age of 25, I publicly accepted Jesus in an Assemblies of God church. I began to share Christ with everyone I knew. My wife, Donna, raised as a Catholic, thought I had flipped my lid. Here was her Jewish husband preaching Jesus to her! I told all my friends and relatives about Him; I even preached to my dog and fish. I was passionate for Jesus.

One woman in the church I was attending told my wife, "Don't worry. He's a fanatic now, but in time he'll calm down and become like the rest of us." Tragically, she was right. Over the course of my television broadcasting career, I did everything I could to reach others with the gospel through the media, but my own relationship with the Lord was pathetically lacking. I didn't realize how lukewarm I had become until I came to Toronto. God was about to turn my life right side up.

As I sat in the service, I realized just how far I had drifted from a personal relationship with God. I had grown cold; the fire was gone. I was like the walking dead! I was no different than my neighbors, who for 22 years had never talked to me about Christ.

The worship time ended and I was deeply touched. My spirit had been stirred. The host walked onto the platform. With the music over, I now saw and heard things that challenged my concept of what was "decent and in order." There were sounds of laughing, groaning and yelling out "Whoa!" I saw people shaking and weeping as the host began talking. A number of people never quite made it back to their seats! They were out cold, lying in the aisles as others stepped over them.

At first it was very hard to concentrate on what the host was saying. Pastor John Arnott began interviewing a man who couldn't stop laughing. He simply asked him, "What was your life like before you came here?" The man tried to speak but then burst out laughing. He composed himself and started again. "Before, I was, I was—" Then he doubled over in hysterics!

Many in the audience began to laugh along with him. At first, I did too. It was very entertaining. But after seven minutes of this, I was getting impatient. Furthermore, I had a problem with what was referred to as "holy laughter." To me it was very rude, especially when people would laugh during a preacher's sermon. After all, it was the Word of God!

I thought to myself, *Okay, let's get on with it already! Talk or just shut up.*

Then, as if he heard my innermost thoughts, the man stopped laughing; and with tears streaming down his face he shared, "Before I came here, I had a gun to my head and was ready to commit suicide."

I wanted to crawl under my seat and cry. I thought, *You jerk, Warren. This man was ready to kill himself! Now God has filled him with joy and laughter. Quit judging! God is here.*

One after another people shared about their marriages being restored and about how the Lord had healed emotional and psychological problems. Many were once spiritually dry and backslidden but now were on fire for God. I was amazed at their testimonies. Pastor John Arnott shared that the evidence that this was God had nothing to do with the manifestations but with the fruit of these testimonies. All of these people loved Jesus more!

Then I noticed a number of people shaking very violently. I turned to Sid and asked, "Are there many healings here?"

He nodded, "Yes, why do you ask?"

"Well, I see a lot of people here with cerebral palsy!"

Sid laughed. "Oh, that's just what happens to some people when the power of God comes on them. Do you want to go up for prayer?"

"No, thanks!" I shot back. I was deathly afraid. I could imagine myself getting prayer and the power of God coming on me, causing me to shake uncontrollably. I wanted no part of it.

The chairs were being stacked against the walls as everyone moved to form straight lines to wait for prayer. The worship leader began to sing more of those intimate songs to the Lord. I walked around the room, observing the scene before me. People were really being affected. Some were crying; others fell to the floor and were shaking. One woman was rolling back and forth on the floor yelling, "Jesus! Jesus! Jesus!" What was this? A psych ward?! It was like the people here had all had a lobotomy. They had checked their brains at the door!

It was then that I spotted Sid Roth. He was laid out on the floor. His face was so peaceful. I complained to God, *Not him, too!* But then I began thinking, *What if this is You, Lord? All these people can't be faking it! Okay, God, I'm going to get some prayer. Give me whatever You want. But please, don't give me that shaking stuff.*

I moved into one of the lines and waited with anticipation. I watched as the prayer team moved down the line closer and closer to me. It seemed that each person they touched was affected even more radically than the one before. My heart began beating hard with expectancy. I closed my eyes and concentrated on the music.

Finally they came to me. There was a prayer team member behind me and another in front of me. The man in front touched me lightly, saying simply, "More, Lord. More!" I stood motionless for an interminable amount of time, and nothing happened. The man said, "Just keep soaking. Someone else will come by and pray for you."

I was extremely disappointed. I mumbled under my breath, "Maybe this is just emotion. God isn't touching these people. If He is, why didn't He touch me?" I opened my eyes and looked around me. I knew that nobody could conjure up the unusual things I was seeing. It was too creative. Nobody in control of himself would want to act so foolishly in front of others. These people didn't care how they looked. They were desperate, and God was doing something in them.

I closed my eyes and began crying out to the Lord, *Oh, God, I need You! I am so sorry for judging others. Please, give me something. If it means shaking, then let me shake. If it means laughing, then let me laugh! There is no way I'm leaving until I get something.* That night I went back to my hotel room without being touched. But I was determined that I was not going to leave Toronto without receiving something from God.

Every night, Sid took me to the church. It seemed that I just couldn't receive.

It was on our last night there that I had a major breakthrough. While standing on the line, a ministry team member came and began praying over me. I started to feel a lightheadedness and a vibrating inside. I thought, *Is this You, God, or is this just my emotions?*

Then my thoughts switched to an image of Jewish men at the Wailing Wall in Jerusalem. They were bowing before the Lord in prayer. They were crying. I asked the Lord, *Why are they praying with such fervency?*

The answer came, "They are lamenting the destruction of the Holy Temple. They are asking, 'Where are You, O God of Israel?'

They are crying out to God to rebuild the Temple again, so that His presence might once again be with them in the Holy of Holies."

My mind drifted and I saw hundreds of people in a large church. Their faces were as intense as the Jewish men I had just seen. They were all weeping. I thought, *They, too, are crying out to God, asking, "Where are You, God? Where is Your presence? There's got to be more. My children are falling away from you. My husband is dying. Oh, Jesus, please come and save us!"*

Tears began to stream down my face. They just kept coming and coming. I couldn't stop crying. I wept for the rest of the night. I was a wreck! Yet I sensed the presence of God so strongly. The fire was rekindled. God had answered my prayer and touched me dramatically. I wanted everyone I knew to taste this! I returned to Lynchburg and began sharing my experience with my family and friends.

It was around the same time that I had been having terrible problems with my teenage daughter, Tara. She was brought up as a Christian. I had sent her to a private Christian school from kindergarten on into high school, but she would tell me that the kids in her school were hypocrites. Unknown to me, Tara was now partying with some of those kids, drinking and smoking marijuana. No matter what I tried to share with her about God, she rejected it. I had lost all hope of reaching her.

I brought back some videos from Toronto and showed them at home. I could see that my daughter was very interested. She told me that if there was a church in Lynchburg like that, she would go. I decided to take her to Toronto.

From the moment we arrived, she loved it. She could relate to the music and felt comfortable with the informal dress. She saw teens her age, passionately pressing into God. When it came time for prayer, Tara went into the prayer lines with me. I anxiously watched as she was prayed for. A ministry team member hardly touched her. She didn't know anything about falling under the Spirit. The next thing I knew, she was on the floor, crying out hysterically to God.

I got frightened and thought, *Maybe I didn't do the right thing. She's going off the deep end now! What's my wife going to say?* For an hour and a half, Tara was on the floor. When she tried to get up, I was there to help her to her feet. I asked her if she was okay. She looked at me with tear-filled eyes and said, "Why didn't anybody tell me there was so much more! Dad, I don't want to be an actress anymore. I want to be a missionary."

I was shocked. She had already decided on her career path. She was to go to the New York University Film School and study acting. I was petrified of that, because I had gone to film school in New York and that is where I began using drugs. Before coming with Tara to Toronto, I had tried everything I could to reach her. But just ONE touch by God and my daughter was instantly on fire for Him! Today she is serving God with her husband, Aaron, who was also touched in Toronto. They lead worship at the Renewal and Revival Center in Lynchburg, Virginia, and are radically in love with Jesus.

My own passion has not eroded; rather, it has exploded. Since 1996, I have been transformed. I can't go through a moment of the day without thinking about God. His presence is so real to me. I can't get enough of Him.

I was so touched by renewal in Toronto that my desire was to let everyone in the world know about this great secret. I brought together some investors and with their help was able to produce a film called *Go Inside the Toronto Blessing,* which documents the wonderful things God is doing through this mighty outpouring. Thousands have been touched through it.

After finishing that film, I wanted to do more to help others experience this revival. I began helping John and Carol Arnott with their weekly TV program, *Catch the Fire*. This half-hour program shares the music, preaching and testimonies of this powerful move of God. It can be seen weekly all over Canada, as well as in some areas of the United States and Europe. My burden to use my filmmaking talents for God's glory also compelled me to produce two other films: *The Smithton Outpouring* and *The Brownsville Revival*.

I was recently ordained as a Southern Baptist evangelist. God has allowed me to preach in Baptist, Methodist, Assembly of God and other denominational churches. The Lord has placed in my heart a passion to share with everyone about the wonderful things He has done for me. I am convinced the Holy Spirit will touch every heart that will put aside pride and judgments and seek Him with a hunger and thirst.

As part of this burden to reach out to our community, we've established the Renewal and Revival Center, 10 miles outside of Lynchburg, Virginia. It is associated with Toronto's Partners in Harvest. The Center is not a church, but a place where people of all denominations can come together in unity and seek God's face. We meet on nights when the church doors are closed. Many continue to be touched and are now helping to spread the fire in their own congregations.

The Lord wants us to be hungry for more of Him. His heart for mankind hasn't changed since the Garden of Eden: He longs to fellowship with us. He wants to be our friend and helper. God loves us and desires that we fall passionately in love with Him. Don't let another day go by without experiencing the fire of revival!

# please don't pass us by

## R. T. KENDALL

*Dr. R. T. Kendall is senior pastor of Westminster Chapel in London. I first met this renowned theologian and author when he came to one of our meetings in Brighton, England, in 1995. His friend and teacher, author Paul Cain, was with him. R. T. watched intently and then incredulously as Paul asked for prayer and was deeply touched by the Spirit of God. Soon after, we were privileged to have R. T. speak at our pastors' conference, and then I was privileged to speak in his prestigious Westminster Chapel in London. Carol and I love the hunger and the integrity of this dear man of God. —J. A.*

I remember it as though it were yesterday. I was sitting with my friends Lyndon Bowring and Charlie Colchester in a Chinese restaurant in Soho, London. As we waited for our food, Charlie asked, "Have you guys heard about this Toronto thing?" Lyndon and I looked at each other quizzically. We hadn't. Charlie continued, "The oddest thing has been happening at our church at Holy Trinity, Brompton. People are falling on the floor and laughing—I've never seen anything like it in my life. Why, last Sunday night we left the church at 11:00 P.M. with about 50 people on the floor! I hated to just leave them there, but we had to go home. What do you think?!" Neither of us was very impressed.

I couldn't stop thinking about it the rest of the evening. I didn't want to believe it was of God, because if God were going to do something great, He would have done it with us at Westminster Chapel first! After all, we had paid the price: We had been out on the streets, witnessing to tramps, beggars, tourists—

anyone who would listen. We had borne the heat of the day; we were the Church trying to reach all of London! Holy Trinity, Brompton, by contrast, was upmarket, posh and Anglo-Saxon. If God were to do something, it would not be in a church like HTB, I reasoned.

I had just had 300 cards printed up for our new Church Prayer Covenant. One of the petitions of the covenant read "We pray for the manifestation of the glory of God in our midst, along with an ever-increasing openness in us to the manner in which God chooses to turn up." I introduced the card the following Sunday and explained the reason for this particular petition.

Sometimes God turns up in strange ways. I knew a little bit of Church history. I knew about the Cane Ridge Revival and how people would sometimes fall and laugh and do odd things. This happened again in the Great Awakening in Jonathan Edwards's day and again in Whitefield's time. So I explained to the congregation that we must allow for God's unusual ways and then used as an example what was going on at HTB. But at the end I added, "I don't believe this *is* of God, but we must be open to the sort of thing God can do." And so I stated publicly that what was going on at HTB was not of God. I was only trying to be honest.

A couple of days later, a group of ministers were meeting at the Westminster Chapel. I went in to greet some of my friends, and there was Lyndon. He introduced me to Bob Cheeseman, pastor of a church near Richmond. Bob had just returned from Toronto, and his face was glowing. I looked at him and said, "Tell me more about it."

He replied, "All I can tell you is that I've never felt Jesus so real in all my life. We just got back from holiday. Usually I will take a novel along, but this time I only wanted to read my Bible. I've never had anything like this happen to me before."

It was the glow on his face that impressed me the most and how he wanted to talk about Jesus that gave me pause. I looked at him and said, "Would you like to come into the vestry and pray for me?" He agreed.

I went back to the vestry and there found a close friend of mine who had come for coffee. He is a Reformed Baptist preacher, well known in London and throughout England. I explained to him that somebody who had just got back from Toronto was going to come in momentarily and pray for me. Then I said to my friend, "You've heard about this Toronto thing?" No, he hadn't.

A moment later Bob Cheeseman knocked on the door, and when he came in, he recognized my friend! They knew each other very well. I said to Bob, "Explain to my friend what happened to you in Toronto." Bob shared with him how he went to Canada, was prayed for and was so blessed that it had spread into his church. Now, my friend had had no conditioning for this sort of thing whatsoever; but he spoke up, "Well, Bob can pray for me, too!" Just then there was a second knock on the door; and yet another minister, Gerald Coates, joined us with "Oh, I want in on this!"

Now, Bob and Gerald were going to pray for me, and just to be courteous, my friend was going to let them pray for him also. They started praying. In less than a minute, my close friend, who had only heard of this phenomenon for the first time moments earlier, fell forward, facedown on the floor! There he was, flat out—and I was sobered. He lay there for about 10 minutes. Finally, he got up and I asked, "What happened to you?"

He replied, "All I know is that I fell, and I couldn't stop it." He later told me that for about a week afterwards, he felt an unusual sense of the presence of God, unlike anything he had known in years.

Next they began to pray for me—all three of them! I took my glasses off because I thought I would be next on the floor. They prayed, but nothing significant happened to me; it had happened to my friend instead. But that day marked a real turning point in my thinking.

A few days later I got a call from Kenneth Costa, a merchant banker and present warden of HTB. He was calling to see if I had any sermons on 1 John 4:1-3 (*NIV*):

Dear friends, do not believe every spirit, but test the spirits to see whether they are from God, because many false prophets have gone out into the world. This is how you can recognize the Spirit of God: Every spirit that acknowledges that Jesus Christ has come in the flesh is from God, but every spirit that does not acknowledge Jesus is not from God. This is the spirit of the antichrist, which you have heard is coming and even now is already in the world.

I did have sermons on the text, and he sent a courier to pick them up. In the meantime he invited me to have lunch with him the following Friday to discuss the sermons and to get my opinion on what was going on in his church. He was slightly troubled by it and seemed to have some trust in me as a Bible theologian.

I went to that lunch fully loaded and ready to explain to him how he must be careful of all this. I was going to persuade him to distance himself from it, although I still could not forget how my friend had so unexpectedly been brought to the floor.

During our lunch, Ken Costa explained that he himself had been touched. He told me about standing up to address a group of men and suddenly being overcome with laughter, so much so that he could not stop himself. He then expressed his concern for sound doctrine and solid teaching. He exhorted, "R. T., your day is coming. This sort of thing is going to need preaching to undergird it and make it sound. So be ready!"

Before we finished, I had a strange feeling that I might be on the wrong side of the issue. I remembered reading that in Jonathan Edwards's day there were those supposedly sound brothers who opposed him. I remembered also that often the very ones who opposed what was happening in the Welsh Revival were also very orthodox. I wondered if I were going to join their ranks!

I feared that I might be moving toward the wrong camp, all because of my pride and my anger that this could happen at Holy Trinity and not at Westminster Chapel. I felt, in fact, that God had betrayed me and let me down. But it was obvious that something *was* happening at HTB. Ken Costa was a man of integrity; I knew that he would not defend anything he did not truly feel was of God.

So then, it was my discussion with Ken, as well as what I observed happen to my friend in the Westminster vestry, which made me reconsider my position. Later that day I said to my wife, Louise, "I think I've been wrong; I have a deep-seated fear that this thing *is* of God." I wrestled with it for a couple of days.

The following Sunday morning, I went into the pulpit and reminded the people of the statement I had previously made about what was happening at HTB. Then I said to them, "I'm afraid that I was wrong. Today I have to climb down: I believe that what is going on there is of God." I reminded them of what I had said so many times before: "What if revival came to All Souls Langham Place or Kensington Temple but not to Westminster—would we affirm it?" I realized now that God was doing something elsewhere and that He had bypassed Westminster Chapel, and I was beginning to be very, very scared that we could miss it entirely.

So I said to the congregation, "I believe something has happened. It is of God, it is going on at Holy Trinity, Brompton, and I would not blame anybody if they wanted to go there and investigate it." Then we bowed our heads and prayed for HTB and for their vicar, Sandy Millar. On that day I nailed my colors to the mast; now everybody knew where I stood.

Many people came around afterward and thanked me for my honesty. Some started attending HTB and we lost members. Others fell out with me because I had affirmed such a thing. One deacon opposed me on it and eventually left the chapel.

A few days later I wrote a letter to Sandy Millar and quoted Acts 16:9, "Come over to Macedonia and help us." I continued, "Please come to Westminster Chapel one evening. I will have all of our deacons and their wives there; I'd like you to bring some of your people and pray for each of us."

He kindly wrote back and agreed to come. We had a buffet supper for our leadership and a dozen of HTB's people. Sandy graciously addressed our deacons for half an hour and then asked that we stand to be prayed for. Three or four of the deacons and one or two of the wives went to the floor, but there was not a lot of laughter or the suchlike. But it was a sacred moment. I was prayed for and felt a weightiness come over me which I could have resisted, but knew that if I did, I'd regret it as long as I lived. I gave in to it and fell forward facedown. I cannot say that there was any great joy or laughter; it was a matter of obedience to the Holy Spirit.

That evening the majority of the men and their wives did not experience any of the unusual manifestations, so I concluded that we had no mandate to push hard for this sort of thing at Westminster. I felt it would be premature at that time. I believe I made the right decision, yet we were now publicly identified with the Toronto Blessing. That was in the summer of 1994.

Not a lot happened immediately after that. We went away on our summer holiday in Florida, and I kept in touch with what was going on in London. It seemed that the Toronto Blessing was spreading like wildfire all over the city and all over England, but it was not coming to the Chapel. I returned in September and decided that I would not do anything to discourage the Toronto Blessing from coming to Westminster, nor would I do anything to work it up or hasten its entrance.

In the meantime I began to have two fears. The first fear was that the Blessing would never come to us and that we would be bypassed altogether. This terrified me. But my second fear was that it *would* come to Westminster and turn our church upside down, throwing us into another crisis. I had been through several crises in the past and was not interested in another one. Still, I was prepared for it if this was the path God would lead us in.

In the following year, my wife and I had the privilege of meeting Rodney and Adonica Howard-Browne. God used them to minister to Louise: She was instantly healed of a serious chronic cough and subsequently released from a three-year depression. Our son also was deeply impacted by their ministry; from him the blessing spread to many of his young friends. In October 1995, Rodney was preaching in London again. About 15 of our people went to hear him speak. Louise and I went over later and found some of our young people on the floor, having been prayed for by Rodney.

The following Sunday night at Westminster Chapel, I invited all who had been to Rodney's meeting to come to the platform and give a testimony. When they finished I turned to the congregation and said, "How many of you would like to be prayed for by these people as well as our deacons?" Nearly every hand went up! That night marked the beginning of the prayer ministry at the chapel. That first evening the praying took place in the church lounge, and it looked like 250 people were trying to squeeze in. A few ended up on the floor but not a lot. There were some manifestations but not many. But a prayer ministry had started unlike anything we had ever experienced before. We have never looked back.

A year later John Arnott came and preached for us. Rather than folding chairs, our church has pews that are fixed to the floor; but this was not an issue for John. People stood in every second row and he prayed for them; great blessing followed. He preached twice that day and the people fell in love with him. His Canadian manner and gentle demeanor endeared him to our congregation and helped them appreciate the authenticity of what was happening; his sermons helped people see how biblical his preaching was.

A special touch of God has come to Westminster Chapel. Although it is not very demonstrative, our prayer ministry still continues. Our deacons anoint the sick with oil according to the pattern given in James 5; we have a special area for prayer for physical healing. Others sit wherever they want in the sanctuary and our prayer ministry team goes and prays for them. We have had a number of miracles, but I don't talk about them a lot because we made a covenant with God several years ago: If He blessed us with signs and wonders, we would not call attention to them; but rather, we would do as the Early Church did—namely, use them as a platform to preach the gospel.

———

Let me briefly share with you something that was absolutely astounding when it happened and still astounds me today. It happened the night I stood up at Toronto Airport Christian Fellowship to preach and could not say a word. It was the second anniversary of the Father's Blessing and the first service in the church under its new name. These people had been disenfranchized from their denomination and could no longer use their previous name.

John Arnott graciously introduced me. I stood up before 4,000 people and made a few introductory remarks. I had decided to preach on Hebrews 4:16, a sermon I had preached over 50 times, so I needed no notes. But as I stood there, I was speechless. I literally could not utter an intelligible or intelligent sentence. *Lord, help me!* I cried out in my heart. I used all the physical and mental energy I could draw on, but I could not preach that sermon. This went on for 15 or 20 minutes. You can order the video and see the whole thing for yourself.

Suddenly, I felt an impulse to turn to Hebrews 13:13 and preach on it. I knew at once that it was God Himself who would not allow me to preach what I knew backwards and forwards. (I have since preached that message on other occasions and did so with ease.)

What did Hebrews 13:13 (*NIV*) say? "Let us, then, go to him outside the camp, bearing the disgrace he bore." I did not grasp the significance of the text until the next day. But that night thoughts poured into my mind extemporaneously. I was at liberty. I was given words. I can't be sure of the number of people who responded to my invitation, but I think the number was between 200 and 300 (including many ministers, I later discovered).

It turned out to be a night of nights for more than one reason. All I know is that God wanted Hebrews 13:13 to be the first sermon preached at Airport Christian Fellowship because He had given them a mandate to go outside the camp.

# there is always enough!

## ROLLAND AND HEIDI BAKER

*Rolland Baker is a third-generation missionary, born in China, whose grandfather wrote the book* Visions Beyond the Veil. *Heidi holds a doctorate degree in theology from King's College at the University of London. They are directors of Iris Ministries and have an orphanage in Maputo, Mozambique. Before this posting, they were missionaries in China, Hong Kong and Indonesia. Over the last five years they have planted out of their Bible training center over 400 churches in Mozambique. My first recollection of this extraordinary couple was when I met Heidi in the upstairs ministry area in our church. I remember being impressed with her hunger as she shared how first her husband had been impacted by the presence of God and then how she also had been powerfully touched. They are perhaps the most dedicated missionaries I have ever met. —J. A.*

I grew up with a wonderful spiritual heritage, as a missionary kid in Asia. My Pentecostal missionary grandfather, H. A. Baker, told me about manifestations of the Holy Spirit, when I was a small boy sitting on his lap. Each time we were together, I would hear more about angels, demons, power encounters, the grace of God, the beauty of Jesus and how people would shake, tremble, fall and cry out when under the power of the Spirit. He told me about revival in his orphanage in China and among the mountain villages of southern Yunnan Province where he faithfully itinerated on foot for 20 years.

His orphans were caught up in visions for days, weeks and even months. While being shown the glories of the New Jerusalem, they would roll on the floor, laugh and shout with joy. They would also weep for the lost and groan over their own sin. My grandfather baptized thousands of new believers in cold mountain rivers. Filled with the Spirit, these baby Christians would come out of the water speaking in tongues. Lost in the things of God, jumping and falling prostrate in worship, physically and emotionally overcome, they received a rich foretaste of the heavenly glories to come.

Through the years I heard about more revivals—in China, Indonesia, South America and in the farthest corners of the world. I got to know people who had raised the dead and had experienced themselves the miracles of the Bible.

I married Heidi, whom I had seen shake and laugh in the Holy Spirit at significant times ever since I first met her more than 20 years ago, and I knew how much she loved God. I kept growing in the love of God myself until I was not surprised by much of anything that people experienced in revival meetings.

When I first heard of the manifestations at the Toronto Airport Church in 1994, I took almost no notice. To me such things were normal—to be expected—when God was moving. My father was not surprised either, as he had seen these things a generation earlier among his friends in my grandfather's ministry. Reports from Toronto seemed to blend naturally into the fabric of revival testimonies that had become our spiritual heritage.

It was not long, however, before Heidi and I realized that what was happening in Toronto was exceptionally wonderful—and controversial. The controversy landed right in the middle of my Ph.D. field of study in systematic theology. I was examining the issue of Word and Spirit and finding out that all through Church history, Christians have been struggling with how to relate God's two ways of revealing Himself: one objectively through the written Word and the other subjectively through experience of the Holy Spirit. This issue concerned me very much, so I immediately began to collect all the information I could about Toronto and what people were saying about it.

My grandfather had dealt with this issue too. Daily he would examine the Bible to sharpen his perception of what was happening in his orphan children and in his mountain churches. He would carefully cross-examine those who told of visions and various revelations, and he would compare their spirits and attitudes with the admonitions of Scripture. There were other missionaries in his part of China who criticized his tolerance of any such experiential enthusiasm, and some actually squelched the work of the Holy Spirit in certain mountain districts where he had worked.

But my grandfather concentrated continually on his preaching and many books on the plain and simple gospel of Jesus Christ and Him crucified. He found that in the children's visions and in all that the Holy Spirit did among his beloved mountain people, Jesus was always glorified, His name was on everyone's lips, and salvation in Jesus was the focus of all the miracles and manifestations.

The events in Toronto showed that for many Christians the issue of Word and Spirit was not resolved at all. Evangelical churches had put a hedge around the Word of God, and it seemed that nearly all experience was suspect. Just as the early Pentecostals were severely criticized and even persecuted for their experience of tongues and other alleged excesses, so now we were hearing of thousands whose testimonies of joy and deliverance at Toronto were being trampled on.

In early 1994, Heidi and I were leading a church for homeless streetsleepers in downtown London where we were also studying for our doctorates at King's College, University of London. By day we would engage astute theological minds and by night we would sit on curbs in the dark and share the good news with the most desperate and poor people we could find. Our church was the testing ground of our understanding.

The more we heard about Toronto, the hungrier we got. The testimonies were too beautiful, the fruit too excellent. We didn't have to be convinced. My whole background had shaped me into a person who wanted everything that God was giving out. Any touch, any word, any revelation, any miracle is to be treasured simply because it is *from Him*.

# heidi speaks

After I heard about the Father's Blessing in Toronto, I was desperate for the Lord to bless our church in London in the same way. We could not afford the airfare to Canada, but I was so starving for more of God that I couldn't stand it. I remember driving around a roundabout in London, crying out to God, "Please, Lord, don't pass us by! We are a church full of street people and we cannot get to Toronto; but please, Lord, move here too. We are desperate; we are hungry; we have to have more of You!"

That Sunday the most amazing thing happened. I prayed that the Lord would pour out His blessing on us just as He was doing in Toronto. The whole church began to cry out to God. Suddenly the Holy Spirit came in great power. People were falling all over the place. One crippled young man began leaping in the air. A city lawyer began rolling on the floor, laughing with incredible joy. Others were weeping in repentance. Lives were transformed and our church was never the same! Those who could afford it flew to Toronto and were powerfully touched. All this made me even more desperate for God.

# rolland speaks

Heidi and I had prayed for years to be sent to the poor. Finally, I visited Mozambique for two weeks in January 1995. Mozambique was listed by the United Nations as the poorest of the world's highly indebted nations. Torn up by decades of war and left with almost no economy or infrastructure, it was an incredible challenge to the gospel. After two days there, I was asked if we wanted an orphanage—a broken-down and vandalized shell of an institution that neither the government nor any aid or mission group would help.

I could never forget my grandfather's ministry and how God used orphans—the very least of these—to reveal Himself to the rest of the world. Would God do the same thing in Mozambique? Would He pour out His Spirit and again bring visions and revelations and transform unwanted street beggars into trophies of His grace?

We said we wanted to take on the children's center, but getting started in Mozambique was not easy. We had to submit many formal proposals to the government. We waited months for a response. Government officials had no faith that we would actually return and do what we said we would do, and we had no financial support for such an operation.

We gained permission to run the orphanage in a joint venture with Mozambique's Department of Education. Heidi arrived in Mozambique in August 1995 and plunged immediately into ministry on the streets and at the center, quickly learning the language as she went. Every day was a battle of faith, but each day the Holy Spirit penetrated further into the hearts of the children.

Meanwhile, I had more Ph.D. research to do in the States. I began to concentrate seriously on Toronto, a perfect case study in my field of interest. To me the theological issues were complex and their discussion had a long history. I imagined detailed interviews and a process of careful investigation. What actually happened was quite different!

First, I temporarily lost interest in my doctoral research. I was just interested in Jesus. After years of theological study and hard missions effort, the prospect of fresh renewal and revival in the company of thousands of others was too much to resist. I couldn't afford the airfare, but Heidi told me to sell the house if necessary and fly to Toronto! We had chosen Jesus for all eternity and we wanted to go for broke.

Toronto's second Catch the Fire conference was coming up in October 1995, so I bought an air ticket in spite of the cost. It was so good to arrive with no other agenda than to seek Him. I was unknown in Toronto and completely free to worship and approach the Lord however I wanted.

I stayed in Toronto for weeks and then came back later for more. I couldn't get enough. How wonderful it was to soak in such an atmosphere without ever getting into a theological argument! Morning, noon and night, all any of us there wanted to do was enjoy Jesus!

My testimony is that when the Holy Spirit is present, the love of God is *felt!* It is so great and so overwhelming. You don't argue; you don't question; and you don't want to think, say or do anything that will diminish that presence or grieve Him.

The goodness of God leads to repentance, and I was so impacted by the Lord's grace that I wept in repentance for hours and then for days—for nearly everything. I wept for joy and I wept in relief. I was excited; I was thrilled. And I was staggered by the purity and power of the grace of God being poured out like a mighty waterfall—so clean, so refreshing and so awesome that nothing could resist it. Receiving God's love was like being lost down in the mist at the base of Niagara Falls, completely awed by the thundering noise, deep currents and brilliant white all around.

When saturated with the Spirit in such an environment, your sensitivity is heightened. Everything is emotionally moving. Everything reflects either God's goodness or the damage Satan has done. Laughing and crying happen all day. Nothing is boring.

Of course I had to share all this with my wife. I called her at 2:00 A.M. and poured out my heart to her into the morning hours. It was the most expensive phone call of my life! I was filled with the deepest love for her and I could hardly wait to get back to Mozambique. Our marriage was at a new level, and that has blessed everything in our ministry.

# heidi speaks

The Lord had shown me clearly that after 12 years in Asia and 3 years in England; now was His time for us to be in Mozambique. But after 16 years of full-time missionary work, I was exhausted.

Each time Rolland and I had relocated from one country to the next, we had felt led to give away everything, including our vehicles and buildings. We had gone to Mozambique with nothing, and we had never tried to raise support or send out appeals. I felt the Lord leading me to pick up hurting, outcast and dying children on the streets of Maputo and, after a few months, I had gathered several hundred of them. It was a challenge to feed the children each day. Corrupt bureaucrats in Mozambique's Department of Education were hassling me daily. Although I was filled with joy to finally be ministering in the poorest nation on Earth, the daily struggles of existence seemed to squeeze all the energy out of me. I was deep-down bone tired.

When Rolland returned from Toronto he was just so nice! He brought me flowers and kept telling me how much he loved me.

I knew I had to get to Toronto myself. Living in such extreme conditions in Mozambique, I often got sick. Once I ended up in the hospital with pneumonia, and as Rolland was visiting me, he opened up a brochure about a pending healing conference in Toronto. I checked myself out of the hospital, much to the doctor's disapproval, and got on a plane.

Our flight stopped in California and I was immediately admitted to the hospital again. I now found it very difficult to breathe. But I was desperately hungry for God; I wanted more of Him than life itself. When I discharged myself from the hospital, the doctors told me they were not responsible for me. I dragged myself onto a plane again, and upon arrival in Toronto I stayed in a rest and renewal home for burned-out missionaries!

During the very first meeting, although I was unable to sing because I couldn't breathe very well, I was overwhelmed by the worship and the presence of God that permeated the place. At one point in the service, I knew that I was totally and instantly healed. I began to breathe normally and to sing and dance. I was filled with incredible joy. When they asked for testimonies, I went forward. I told them what God had done, and then members of the prayer team began to pray for me. As they did, God completely blasted me! I was on the floor for hours.

I saw a vision of Jesus. I saw His face. I saw His burning eyes of love piercing through my soul. I saw His broken, bruised body. There were thousands of children surrounding Jesus. I began to weep and I cried out, "No, no, there are too many!"

The Lord replied, "Look into my eyes." My heart melted as I looked into His face. He handed me a piece of His broken, bruised body and said, "Give it to them to eat." His body became bread in my hands. I gave it to all of the children and everyone ate. Jesus said, "I died so that there would always be enough."

Again He said, "Look into my eyes," and He handed me a cup of blood and water that flowed from His side. I knew it was a cup of bitterness and joy. At first I drank it; then I gave it to the children to drink and they all drank their fill. Once more He said, "I died so that there would always be enough."

After you see His face, you can never be the same. From that day forward, I have never said no to a single orphan or to an abandoned or dying child. I simply take them all. And as He promised, there has always been enough.

At the conference, during a special meeting for pastors, Toronto staff member Sharon Wright asked if she could pray for me. It was the most anointed, healing prayer I had ever received. She held me in her arms and quietly ministered God's heart to my wearied, exhausted life. I knew that Father God loved me for who I was and not for what I did. And I was deeply changed. There are no words to describe how much that time meant to me. She must have prayed for me for over an hour. I've never experienced someone praying such a long time for me. I learned about soaking prayer and I have since become a soaker.

When I got home, I expected everything to change. I couldn't wait to see thousands of children in the center. I began making plans to build more dorms. But several weeks after my return, we were issued a 48-hour eviction notice. Marxist factions in the Department of Education told us we could not worship God on government property. We were devastated. We had no place to go with 320 children. I learned there was a $20 contract on my life (I've always said I was worth more than $20!). Rolland and I and our two children had to escape during the night without our belongings.

Our hundreds of children defied the government directors and began to sing and worship in the cafeteria. They were beaten with sticks, and rocks were thrown at their heads. They began to walk barefoot the 15 miles to our little office in town. When they would arrive, they would say, "We want to stay with you, Mama!" I said, "There is no place to go!" But they would reply, "You said there is always enough!"

After several days of children drifting in, there were over 100 children living everywhere in our little office with one toilet. Because we had lost everything, including our pots and pans, we hadn't eaten in days. A friend from the embassy called to say she was bringing over chili and rice for our family. When she arrived, I told her we had a really big family. She said, "No, no, I made this for your family of four!" I opened the door and showed her all the children and said, "Jesus told me there's always enough!"

She was upset and wanted to go home and make more food. But I had a bit of cornmeal and her pot of chili and rice. I told all the children to sit down and pulled out the plastic bowls and began filling them up. Every single child ate. Then Rolland and I and Crystalyn and Elisha ate too. God multiplied the food. There is always enough if we see His face.

Shortly after we lost the center, I was invited to preach at a large Stateside church where they promised us $1 million to build our children's center. I was thrilled. What a great provision from God! But upon our arrival we received a letter from this church stating that all support would be immediately dropped if we were associated in any way with the renewals in Toronto or Pensacola.

Rolland and I had a big decision to make. We already had hundreds of children who called us Mom and Dad, and we desperately needed another center. We were living in tents and in deplorable conditions. We decided to head up to Toronto and sneak into the back of their Have Another Drink conference. As theologians we were going to determine if all this was worth losing our funding.

During the first meeting, John Arnott asked if there was a couple from Mozambique present. We were horrified because we had been told not to be there! We looked at each other and wondered what to do; then we slowly stepped out of our seats at the back of the building and went up front. Well, that was the end of me. We shared our testimony briefly and then I got completely blasted. Electricity went through my body and the power of God hit me like a lightning bolt. Carol Arnott prayed for me for a long time. I shook, I cried, I rolled, I bounced and I laughed as I was overwhelmed by the presence and love of God. Rolland later joked that it was not a great way to stay incognito!

God's presence was so wonderful. He met us in meeting after meeting. We were restored, motivated and encouraged. All the weariness melted away. We had come to that meeting having lost everything and wanting to quit missionary work. Instead, we were tremendously empowered for service.

During the conference I received another life-changing vision. I saw the wedding feast of the Lamb. There were huge, long tables laid out with the most beautiful food I have ever seen. I heard the Lord say, "Wake up, Church! Wake up, Church! The feast is about to begin! The poor have not yet been called and My house is not yet full. I want My house to be full!"

Then I saw the Lord Jesus dancing on the garbage dump, and I was with Him. As He called, the children and youth began to follow and dance with us. Together, Jesus and I would stop and touch them; and their bloated bellies would become flat, and their infected wounds healed. Their hair, turned brown by malnutrition, would become black and shiny. He put beautiful garments of purple, blue, gold and silver on them. He led them out of the dump and into the wedding feast and said, "You sit in front!" And the hungry children from the garbage dump sat at the head table. I've worked in the garbage dump ever since, and many hundreds of children and youth there have met the Lord and are being fed physical and spiritual bread.

We returned to Mozambique encouraged and refreshed. Our work was progressing and our children were responding to the Lord. He would visit them in special ways. Some were taken up to heaven where they would dance with the angels and sit on the Lord's lap. He would speak to them about their lives and their callings. We planted two churches near the capital city of Maputo and were blessed by all that God was doing.

In January 1998 we returned to Toronto for a pastors' conference where John Arnott and Randy Clark were speaking. John was speaking about the anointing and the weight of the glory of God. In one meeting, without anyone touching me, God's presence fell on me like a heavy blanket of liquid love. I was unable to move. I couldn't lift my head, and Rolland had to carry me everywhere. I was on the floor for days. The precious staff at Toronto were very sensitive to the fact that God's presence was on me. They provided a prayer room where I could be alone with God. I was barely able to speak, and Rolland came with me into the prayer room. The awesome and holy presence of God was so thick.

I asked Rolland to read Scriptures that God was impressing on me. As he read them, it was as if the words were directly entering my heart. I saw things in the Word I had never understood before. The Lord spoke to me about unity in the Body of Christ and about how important it is for His Body to be one. He spoke to me about being an imitator of God and about living a life of love—just as Christ Jesus loved us and gave Himself up for us as a fragrant offering and sacrifice to God. He spoke to me about laying down my life as a living sacrifice and about living a life of total purity, set apart for Him alone. He talked to me about the fruit of the Spirit, about my relationship with Rolland, and about my relationship with my children and our coworkers. He was transforming my way of thinking. I put on the whole armor of God. Nothing would ever be the same.

In one session Randy Clark preached on dying to self and the holy fire of God. When he spoke on pressing in, I couldn't stay in my seat. I didn't care what anyone thought. I was so desperate for more of God that I ran forward and knelt at the altar. The fire of God hit me, and I felt like I was literally going to burn up and die. I began to cry out, "I'm dying, I'm dying!" I heard the Lord say, "Good, I want you dead!" Not knowing who I was, Randy grabbed my hand and told me there was an apostolic anointing on my life. He declared that I would see the blind healed and many miraculous healings. He asked me, "Do you want the nation? God's giving you a nation." I cried out, "Yes!" and for hours the power of God flowed through my body like an electric current.

Then I heard the Lord say, "You'll have hundreds of churches!" I began slapping the floor and laughing. It was the funniest thing I had ever heard! It had taken us 18 years to plant four churches. How could there ever be hundreds? But I knew I had heard the Lord.

When we returned to Mozambique, I changed my leadership style dramatically. I delegated more to others. I began pouring my heart into training national leaders. We started to plant new churches and we established a Bible college. Although I am not a strategic planner, God would drop strategies into my heart. Our Bible college runs in three-month sessions through the year so that full-time pastors can receive intensive training before they return to their churches.

During the first session, the power of God hit the 20 pastors attending. I prophesied over two of them that they would raise the dead. I told them to pray for every dead person they could find. When they returned to the Bible school for the next session, they reported to me that five people had been raised from the dead! Glory to God! There is explosive growth in our churches as our pastors are filled with the presence and power of God.

Randy had prayed over me several times that I would see the blind gain their sight, the crippled walk, the dumb speak and the deaf hear. I began praying for every blind person I could find. I knew God would fulfill His promise. When I went to the north with my fellow worker Tanneken and one of our Mozambican pastors, we prayed for a lady who was totally blind. Her eyes were white. She fell over under the power of God and her eyes turned from white to gray to brown. She could see!

We prayed for a boy who was unable to speak, set him free from demonic power in Jesus' name, and he began to speak fluently. Several who could not hear had their hearing restored. The power of God changed many lives and entire villages were saved. We began to develop small groups and released our children and youth to preach with us on the streets and in the garbage dump. Church planting became so easy. The brand-new Mozambican pastors were given supernatural wisdom and power. Two hundred churches were planted that year! God had fulfilled His promise.

When we returned to Toronto after joining Partners in Harvest, the Lord began to put more strategies into my heart. During the 1999 Partners conference, He told me that by that time the following year there would be over 400 churches established! I didn't know how it could possibly happen. And again the presence of God was so strong on me that I was unable to walk for days. Finally John Arnott rented a wheelchair for me!

When we returned to Mozambique, I knew God was up to something. I was wondering how we would see 400 churches by October 2000. What happened next was something no one could ever have expected. On February 7, massive flooding hit Mozam-

bique, marking the worst natural disaster in the nation's history.
One million people were left homeless. Many died.

During the floods the Lord spoke to my heart and confirmed to our staff that we should feed 5,000 people. At the time
we had $27 in our local bank. We already had to feed over 600
people a day. It seemed ridiculous and impossible to feed 5,000
people, but the Lord had said, "There is always enough!" He was
always stretching us beyond our ability. I felt like I was stepping
out of the boat and onto the water. If I would fix my eyes on
Jesus, nothing would be impossible. We committed to feed
5,000, and later 10,000, people a day with freshly baked loaves of
bread. I can testify that there has always been enough!

Since the floods we have moved into revival. It used to take
us four or five days to reach one village of perhaps 100 people.
But because of the disaster, thousands and thousands of people
were brought together in camps. Every day we were able to send
out teams of medical doctors, preachers and aid workers on
United Nations helicopters. Within less than an hour, we would
be flown into camps where thousands were hungry to hear the
gospel. In six weeks I was able to lead over 12,000 people to the
Lord! Again God was fulfilling His promise. Churches are being
planted in new areas at the rate of two churches every week!

The Lord is pouring out His power and His presence in
Mozambique. The people are physically and spiritually hungry,
and every day the Lord is providing bread for their bodies and
for their souls. Blessed are the poor in spirit, for theirs is the
kingdom of heaven (see Matt. 5:3).

By October 2000, there will be over 400 churches in
Mozambique! In 20 years of missionary work I have never seen
such hunger. There is fresh bread in God's house, and it's time
for the poor to be called to the wedding feast. There is always
enough.

# act justly, love mercy, walk humbly

### RALPH A. BEISNER

*Ralph Beisner is a New York State Supreme Court judge. I learned that he had come from New York with three friends from his church to investigate for himself what had precipitated the wonderful and profound change in his wife, Inger. I was amazed to hear him share from our platform how God had touched him. He went home from Toronto never to be the same again. —J. A.*

In 1995, I was an elected New York State Supreme Court Justice. I had been a trial lawyer for about 25 years. I was used to presenting and scrutinizing evidence to determine the validity of the facts. I seldom took the testimony of a person at face value. A lawyer examines motivation, presentation and myriad other factors before accepting what is told to him or her. Then there is always another side to the story. I guess trial lawyers are cynical by nature, and I fit the stereotype!

In addition to working as an attorney, I had just finished serving as an elder in a strong evangelical church. We had a congregational form of church government and had gone for extended periods without a full-time minister. Pastors who tried to exert their leadership were viewed with alarm by the congregation and dismissed. As a result, the elders served in many of the ministerial functions. It often fell upon me to preach the Word on Sunday mornings.

I remember discouraging people from getting too emotional in their worship. Dancing, raising hands and rising to one's feet were all frowned on. I distinctly recall asking a mother to restrain her five-year-old daughter from dancing during worship; it interfered with the orderly invocation of our proper, unemotional God! One of my successors observed that we invited the Holy Spirit into our church but frisked Him at the door.

Yet the Lord had a purpose for my time there. I had to really dig into the Word of God to prepare my sermons. It was similar to preparing a case for a jury. I had to examine and believe what I was saying in order to make a credible presentation. Those years were a time of intense preparation. I emerged from that experience with a deep knowledge of the written Word of God, but I knew nothing of His power!

In early 1995, I left the elder board of my church. I was coming under attack on several fronts. My health seemed to be deteriorating. I was 52 and felt every bit of it. My professional capabilities were being questioned. The church I had served was in turmoil, having just released another pastor. "God, there must be more than this!" was a constant cry from my lips.

# toronto

That April, I was presiding in Manhattan and living there during the week. My wife, Inger, took the opportunity to visit a friend's church in Vermont. They were hosting something called a renewal conference, and people from a church in Toronto were ministering.

When Inger returned, she came down to New York City and stayed with me. We had planned on taking advantage of the theaters and restaurants of the city. She tried to tell me of her experience at the conference. I remember thinking that it was easy for her to get so excited about God—she didn't have to deal with the world like I did. She actually had compassion for the homeless people we encountered on the streets. I figured it was a passing phenomenon and would play itself out over time.

She urged me to get a copy of *Catch the Fire* by an author named Guy Chevreau. Because I was away from home, I had a lot of time to read. I finished the book in a few sittings and remember thinking, *Could this be true? Would God really intervene in our lives today with healing and words of knowledge? Would He really shake His people and change their lives? Would He really have a dialogue with me?* The stage was being set.

Inger continued to tell our home Bible study group about this renewal experience she had encountered in Vermont. She urged me and the other men in the group to travel to Toronto and see for ourselves. Guy Chevreau's book and Inger's testimony were strong incentives to go and check it out, although I still made all the usual prideful objections: "The Bible says the Holy Spirit lives in me. My God can come and meet me right here in my church; I don't have to go to Canada to experience Him!"

Having been married for 30 years, I knew that the only way I was going to pacify my wife was to make plans to travel to this church in Toronto. I suspected it was part of some really weird, fringe group. I told Inger that I would go but not with her. I was a streetwise trial attorney, and I didn't want my observations and conclusions tainted by her expectations.

It was a sunny Friday morning in August when, together with three friends from the church, I got in the car for the eight-hour drive to Toronto. We were going to check this out and reach our own conclusions.

When we arrived, we knew something was different. People were standing in line outside the church! When the doors were finally opened, they pressed one another to get in. I was more accustomed to people jostling to exit a church, not to enter it!

We found four seats together and agreed that we would give each other the freedom to participate to whatever extent each felt comfortable.

The music started. There were drums and guitars—this was very different for us. People seemed to be getting into the worship. We stood to our feet very tentatively and began clapping our hands. This was good!

A pastor got up and delivered a typical message of encouragement from Scripture. Nothing too radical here, except that he invited his wife to also speak from the pulpit. We could overlook that. What she had to say was sound and supported by the Word. We later learned that the regular staff was away on vacation, and the speaker and his wife were from a church near our home in New York.

The really unusual part of the meeting came after the sermon. Everyone was invited to go to the back of the auditorium and stand on taped red lines to receive something called ministry prayer from designated volunteers. I figured I would just stay seated along with my buddies and watch all these other people participate in this mass emotionalism. Besides, I didn't have anything really important that needed God's immediate attention. The next moment, my three friends jumped up and ran to the back of the hall to stand on the red lines! I held my place. After all, I had been their elder and I was the oldest of the group: I had to maintain a certain image.

After about 30 minutes I wandered toward the rear and came across the youngest member of our group, a 17-year-old. He had a grin from ear to ear. I asked him what had happened. Laughing, he told me he had been knocked off his feet by some spiritual force. I asked where our other two fellow travelers were. He told me they were still on the floor and he was going back to stand on the red lines again. I didn't feel comfortable about going to the lines, so I just went to the front where the band was playing and tried to enter into the worship. I smiled as I saw the enthusiasm of the many young people that were there. They were dancing and singing with such abandon!

We stayed for the Saturday evening and the Sunday morning services. I eventually found my way to the red lines. Members of the ministry team prayed for me. Nothing happened. But I did enjoy the music and the freedom of the worship.

On the drive home Sunday afternoon we all began to recognize that something was different. There was a great deal of joy. We found ourselves praying for people and circumstances. One fellow had begun to jerk and speak in tongues at the Sunday morning service. This continued in the car! I, on the other hand, felt like I was looking at the world through different eyes. All of God's creation seemed more beautiful. This was true even as we drove through urban factory areas. I didn't see the grime and decay, I only saw God's goodness, grace and mercy. God had touched each one of us that weekend—each in the unique way we needed.

I called Inger from the thruway and asked her not to go to bed until I got home and had a chance to talk to her. When I arrived, I apologized for not taking her more seriously when she witnessed to me of her renewal experience. That night God began to form a deeper relationship between us that would allow us to be used by Him in ways we couldn't have imagined.

When I went to work the next Monday, my law clerk said to me, "What happened to you?"

"Nothing happened to me," I replied.

"Something happened to you!" she said. "You look like a Christian."

Wow! I wondered what I must have looked like before. I didn't think I had visibly changed. To people who knew me, however,

I had. That day over lunch I had the opportunity to witness the renewal experience to her.

# catch the fire conference, 1995

In October 1995, the second annual Catch the Fire conference was being held at a hotel in Toronto. Inger and I had planned to take a vacation in Italy during that time. Again she prevailed on me to change our plans so we could attend this conference. Spending five or six days with a group of religious fanatics was not high on my list of great vacations! But I gave in and we were off to Toronto.

At the end of one meeting I volunteered to "catch" for some of the ministry team. This gave me a firsthand opportunity to see exactly what was happening. I saw nothing suspect. No one was being pushed over. Actually, the prayer team members were very gentle. The people who did fall over were clearly having a strong emotional or spiritual experience. Yet every time someone prayed for me I stayed standing, just like an oak!

During the first few meetings I had a sense that I should tell the leadership that I was a judge. I tried to ignore this prompting. It was probably my ego that was urging me. Besides, I was here as a Christian, not as a judge. On Friday morning the speaker urged that if God was speaking to us, we should listen. Was God telling me to disclose my profession? I doubted it.

There were forms available for people to submit their testimonies. I decided I would fill one out and that would take care of the matter. In a very cursory manner I told the events of the previous August and threw the document into a basket that contained hundreds of forms. I had done my duty and doubted I would ever hear about it again. Wrong!

My testimony found its way into the hands of the Toronto leadership, and following the worship in the Friday night meeting, Pastor John Arnott called out my name in front of the thousands of people who had gathered. I went up front with Inger. I gave witness to the experiences of the previous summer and shared how God had impacted my life. The leaders on the platform prayed for me and I went down like a stone! God had wanted me to swallow my pride and listen to His voice. When I submitted to Him, He blessed me!

The rest of the conference is a blur. I do remember being physically thrown around by the Holy Spirit on Saturday night. When I got up off the carpet, there was a line of people asking me to pray for them. Me! Again I had learned that if God wanted me to do something, I should do it and He would bless it. I prayed for the people. They began to fall over. I was amazed that He would use me.

# pressing in

In the years since the events of 1995, my life has changed dramatically. I was reelected to a second 14-year term in office by a greater margin than the first election, even though the demographics of the district had changed and were not in my favor.

I was diagnosed twice with different cancers. While I was lying on the operating table at Albany Medical Center, being prepared for extensive surgery, the Holy Spirit told me, "Rejoice and rejoice again!" (see Phil. 4:4). He also told me that the joy of the Lord is my strength (see Neh. 8:10). Joy was not an emotion I was feeling, but I knew that He is a God of miracles. Jesus cured me and continues to heal me of the cancer; He just used the doctors to perform His will.

My relationship with my wife, children and grandchildren is deeper and richer than ever. My perspective on the people who come before me in court has changed. I now look with compassion and understanding on them and the circumstances that bring them before me. Through this renewal experience my life has taken on a depth and quality that was lacking prior to that August weekend in 1995. Scriptures such as "mercy triumphs over judgment" (James 2:13, *NIV*) and "proclaim freedom for the prisoners" (Luke 4:18, *NIV*) are unusual concepts for a judge. In a spiritual sense, however, there is no inconsistency. Being a judge is what I do, not who I am. Through this renewal the Lord has spoken to me through Micah 6:8 *(NIV)*, which exhorts us "to act justly and to love mercy and to walk humbly with your God."

Through contacts we have made at the Toronto Airport Christian Fellowship, Inger and I have been privileged to minister in Italy and Mexico. That vacation in Italy, which I gave up in the fall of 1995, was returned to me exceedingly abundantly, more than I could ever hope or ask for! Furthermore, we have spoken in and witnessed the goodness of God through this renewal in several churches in New York State, and have seen God's healing and deliverance more times than we can count.

# the future

A continuing question over the past several years has been why. Why has God chosen to pour forth His love in this phenomenon called renewal? I'm sure that theologians would have many theories about this; for me it is as simple as this: The function of the Church is to train and equip the saints for the work of the ministry (see Eph. 4:12). Through this renewal, God continues to prepare each one of us to be carriers of His good news to those who will never set foot in a traditional church. You and I, His renewed and strengthened people, will move with the power of the Holy Spirit among the nations of this world. We are the ones He will use to heal, prophesy and proclaim freedom to the captives!

> The harvest is plentiful but the workers are few. Ask the Lord of the harvest, therefore, to send out workers into his harvest field (Matt. 9:37,38, *NIV*).

# a holy disturbance

### GRANT W. MULLEN

*Grant Mullen, a physician practicing in Grimsby, Ontario, was of special interest to me because of his specialization in mental health. Here is a knowledgeable witness who understands emotional excess and hysteria, yet he began sending some of his patients to our meetings because of the deep healing they were receiving here. Since his encounter with the Holy Spirit, Grant has been launched into a whole new area of ministry. Today he writes and lectures widely on how medical treatment, deliverance and the inner healing of life's wounds all work together to break the chains of emotional bondage through the Spirit's power. His book* Why Do I Feel So Down When My Faith Should Lift Me Up? *explains the medical, spiritual and emotional paths to personal recovery. —J. A.*

I was raised in a very conservative Pentecostal home. We were committed to the truth of God's Word but avoided any emotionalism. I accepted Christ at about age seven, because it just seemed like a logical thing to do living in a Christian home. As a teenager I had the experience of speaking in tongues. It was my understanding at the time that tongues was the pinnacle experience in God and, after that, there was nothing further to seek. I then settled into maintenance mode. Being an academic type and a physician, I preferred an intellectual style of Christianity that was focused on truth, not experience. I was quite happy that the "old-time religion" had disappeared so that my denomination could gain respectability in the broader evangelical community. I carefully avoided all emotionalism and even became destructively critical of loud or emotional preachers.

Throughout this process my heart became hardened. I was frozen into a dry, lifeless faith that was grounded in truth but had little fruit. I became much like an intolerant, critical, know-it-all Pharisee.

# the transformation

I continued this way until about 1990 when, through my work in mental health, I began to uncover disturbing experiences that both my Christian and secular patients were having. These incidents did not fit into a medical framework, and I suspected that they could be occult events with a demonic origin. My merely intellectual curiosity with these phenomena changed dramatically when one day a voice spoke out of one of these patients and said, "Leave her alone; she's ours." On that day I realized there was far more to spiritual reality than I had been aware of. In that situation, head knowledge was not good enough. Spiritual power and experience were required, and I knew little of either. From that day, God birthed in me a spiritual hunger for more supernatural reality in my Christian walk.

At this same time, the church I was attending was really struggling. It had been through several traumatic experiences. There had been little growth for many years; finances were so bad that we lived in constant fear of losing our building to the bank. My pastor, Terry Bone, was becoming exhausted. After two years of valiant effort, the church was not improving. He felt that his ministry effectiveness was at a maintenance level and that he was suffering from a "power shortage" after expending so much energy trying to keep the church afloat. (Terry tells his story in Guy Chevreau's book *Catch the Fire*.)[1]

In January 1994, we heard of the strange meetings taking place at the Toronto Airport Christian Fellowship. My brother, who is also a physician in my office, went immediately to the meetings and reported to me that this was the most significant spiritual phenomenon he had ever seen. I, the consummate Pharisee, dismissed the matter as just another emotional binge for flaky Christians. I didn't give it another thought.

My pastor was also being encouraged to attend the meetings by people he respected. We both, however, trusted in that famous religious axiom: "If God wants to touch us, He can reach us where we are. We don't have to travel anywhere; we will not run after other people's blessings." This of course is just a way of covering up denominational pride and spiritual jealousy.

Fortunately, Pastor Terry's hunger for God and frustration with our situation overcame that pride and jealousy, as well as the fear of disorderly worship. He bravely attended a morning pastors' meeting at TACF. He was warmly welcomed, prayed for and prophesied over until he felt a heavy presence of the Holy Spirit slide him off his chair and onto the floor. After some time lying on the floor, having peculiar sensations and enjoying the presence of God, he got up and returned home. At that point he felt no particular change in himself.

That evening he led a Sunday School picnic planning meeting with 12 teachers, including my wife, Kathy. These planning meetings were the least anointed events on the church calendar. The purpose was to assign tasks and go home. After the business was completed, Terry began a closing prayer. In the middle of the prayer, God spoke to him and said, "There's work to do." As the group waited in prayer, powerful physical manifestations began to take place. People began to weep, dance, laugh and fall on the floor. This went on for 90 minutes!

Everyone present was shocked. From that day, the power of the Holy Spirit, with physical manifestations, has been present at each church service.

Even the children's program has been affected. On several occasions when I have gone downstairs to collect my children at the end of a Sunday evening service, I have found my seven-year-old daughter and other children lying all over the floor, speaking in tongues and trembling under the power of the Holy Spirit.

The entire church was shaken by these events. We wondered what was happening. Many members fled the church in fear of demonic infiltration or out of discomfort with the manifestations. Those who had experienced the manifestations reported that their lives had been transformed. Emotions were healed and relationships were restored. Their faith and love for God increased as well as their desire to pray and worship. People loved to come to church and didn't want to go home.

## A Difficult Decision for the Church

This major disruption in the church caused great concern among the members and forced the leadership to make a very difficult decision. On the one hand, we were seeing strange supernatural activity, which was transforming lives. On the other hand, we were now losing frightened members! This meant the church income was dropping. As I mentioned, we lived on the edge of mortgage default every month. We could not afford to lose even one tithe. At one of the most significant leadership meetings I have ever attended, the dilemma was placed before the leaders who had remained. Was this new phenomenon from God? Would we allow it to continue? Could the church survive financially if we continued to lose members? We had to seriously weigh the recent events and address the many objections to what was happening. There were several key questions that we struggled with.

Was this scriptural? Many felt that God would not behave this way and make us uncomfortable. We found many examples in the Bible where people reacted in dramatic ways when God's supernatural presence appeared. The disciples were shaken, the shepherds were terrified, Paul was knocked off his horse, and many feared for their lives. That's probably why the angels so often started their messages with the words "Fear not." In most situations the Holy Spirit's arrival was unexpected and dramatic, causing quite a disturbance. In Acts 2, the fire of the Holy Spirit descending on the believers on the Day of Pentecost caused them to behave in ways that made onlookers suspect they were drunk. That event likely made other believers uncomfortable and, perhaps, ashamed of their leaders, yet 3,000 were saved in a single day!

We concluded that God did not always act in a decent and orderly way and that we should not exclude the possibility that He could visit our church and cause quite a disturbance. Could we as leaders accept such a visitation? We had to examine the fruit of these experiences; in most cases we saw transformed lives and increased love for God.

I had to ask myself, *Wasn't salvation or even tongues enough supernatural experience? Did I need anything else?* Again I had to examine the fruit. After my experience with tongues as a teen, there was no noticeable change in my life, other than a sense of relief that I had finally arrived and no longer had to feel badgered by ministers. My friends, however, who were having such strange physical manifestations, were experiencing life-changing emotional and spiritual transformations. It appeared to me that God did not just want us to be saved, but He also wanted us to be transformed.

Was this phenomenon man-made or fleshly? At that time only the pastor and one other church member had visited TACF.

We couldn't conclude that all the people in our congregation who were involved were just imitating what they had seen at TACF. No special speaker or evangelist had "brought" or hyped the events. Everything had happened suddenly, unexpectedly and spontaneously. There was no doubt that flesh was involved since everyone was responding in slightly different ways. We concluded that the physical manifestations were the human flesh's response to the supernatural presence and power and, therefore, would be unique to each individual. I felt that the manifestations were just like a flashing yellow light at a construction site, indicating "God at work." If fleshly responses were to be eliminated from the church, we would have to ask everyone to leave and just preach to empty pews.

Were the manifestations of a demonic origin? There was no doubt that we were seeing more demonic manifestations than ever before. Sometimes they were happening right beside someone with godly manifestations. This was confusing to us. We eventually concluded that the power of God was both blessing people and exposing their demonic bondages. But better for a demon to be exposed and removed than for it to remain in hiding and never be dealt with! It took some time and experience to discern which manifestations were from God, the flesh or Satan.

We had faced the major objections and answered these questions to the best of our limited understanding. We decided that these recent events were, in fact, from God—an answer to our prayers for the church's awakening. We committed ourselves to following the Holy Spirit wherever He would take us and whatever the cost. We verbally repented for trying to control and limit God in the past, and we gave the leadership of the church back to the Holy Spirit. We acknowledged that we could lose our building and our financial foundation, but it was more important to follow God and obey Him. This unanimous decision was a turning point in the history of our church. Now the pastor had the freedom to lead and to establish the church's identity in this new "river." We would never be the same again.

## What About Me?

Up to this point, I was a spectator of the amazing things God was doing in my church and my family. I endorsed the changes at church, but the fresh move of the Spirit had not touched me personally. Because I was such a reserved person, I was not in a hurry to experience the physical manifestations, but I saw the transformations in my friends and relatives. I knew that I needed such a touch from God. As I watched the Holy Spirit work in my church week after week, I developed a strong hunger for more of God, a hunger that finally overcame my conservative personality. I decided that I wanted this empowering experience so badly that I didn't care what I looked like.

I never missed an opportunity to be prayed for in my church, but nothing happened. Month after month passed, and I became known as one who was "hard to receive." Even my pastor became discouraged with my lack of response when all around me people would be receiving powerfully. (Because I had become such a large block of ice spiritually, it took a long time to thaw me out!)

In my fourth month of seeking, I had a life-transforming experience. One Sunday night as Kathy was heading out to church and I was staying home with our small children, God revealed to me that I had been carrying a bitterness for 10 years. He showed me that it was destroying me and that I needed to let it go. I mentioned this to Kathy as she left. I then went to my bedroom to pray about the matter and make things right. As I walked around my room, praying, I felt a gentle weight or pressure descend over my head and shoulders, and my legs began to get weak. I lay down on the floor because it was not safe for me to continue to walk. Within moments of being on the floor I began to shake and feel the power of God all over me. This went on for one hour; then I had to pry myself off the floor and put the kids to bed. I, of course, was not in church. No one was praying for me and there was no music, no catcher, no prayer lines marked out on the floor. There was no hype or hysteria and no one suggesting I should fall. It was just God and me. I knew this was real.

That night, Kathy was very late coming home from church. This was not too surprising since our church services were getting longer and prayer ministry times had become so exciting that no one wanted to go home. Eventually I heard a clamor in my driveway and a ring at the front door.

When I opened the door, two of our elders carried in my wife, who was trembling so much that she could not safely walk or drive! It was clear that as God had set me free of bitterness and then visited me with the power of the Holy Spirit, Kathy was having a similar experience at church. The chain that had come off me had come off her too.

In the days that followed, there was an immediate and noticeable change in my attitude, personality and love for God. I was happier, more relaxed, more tolerant and worshipful. The presence of God was noticeable in the house and mild physical manifestations of the Holy Spirit became commonplace in our home.

## The Great Challenge

Within a month, a friend who was pastoring a small church asked if I would come and preach on a Sunday morning and tell the congregation what was happening at our church. Word had spread that our church was becoming like TACF. I had never preached before, so this invitation was terrifying. I had often done missions education slide presentations in churches, but that was not preaching. To make matters worse, I didn't really understand what was happening at my church and I still had not even visited TACF. I had no idea what to say.

Then he called and asked if I would pray for people after my message so that they could receive too! Now I was overwhelmed. I had never prayed for anyone in church and was only a few weeks into my own renewal experience. He obviously wanted a John Arnott to visit. He clearly had the wrong person. I had less than a week to respond and prepare for this. I cried out to God for an answer. Within two days He had my daughter's first-grade teacher, whom I had never met, call my wife with a prophetic word for me. This word clearly directed me to proceed with the meeting and just report on what I'd seen. I now knew what I was to do but still didn't know what I was to say. I quickly studied the book *Catch the Fire*, so I would know what was going on at TACF and how they were trying to explain it.

When I finally got up to preach that Sunday morning, I was terrified. The small congregation had high expectations, and I didn't know what I was doing. After a simple report of what God had done at my church and at TACF, I asked if anyone wanted to come and be prayed for to receive a new touch from God. I didn't know what I was going to do if anyone came forward, but I had often watched my pastor do this and I had been prayed for many times.

Well, to my horror, almost the whole church came forward! I approached the first person—a woman—closed my eyes in fear and just repeated the prayer I had heard so many times: "Come, Holy Spirit." Within moments there was no one touching my hands. I opened my eyes and, to my absolute astonishment, saw her crumpled on the floor! I moved on to the next person and the same thing happened. People just kept falling over, so Kathy had to run forward and be my catcher. It was an incredible time as God touched His hungry people. I learned that day that God responds to hunger, not to anything clever that I could ever do or say.

# the two phases of renewal

As I have watched this move of God mature over the past six years, it is clear to me that the primary fruit of this outpouring is emotional transformation leading to a deeper love for God. I continue to be astonished at the rapid transformation in some of my mental health clinic patients after they have experienced the touch of the Holy Spirit. I have referred many patients to TACF for prayer ministry as a supplement to their medications.

The emotional transformation I have observed often seems to have two phases. Initially there is what many call the "gentle rain" phase. This is when the Holy Spirit comes to refresh and renew our hearts, rekindle our love for God and heal many of our attitudes. This process softens the soil of our hearts so that we can receive more of God's reviving love.

If we are serious about following God along the path of renewal and if we permit Him to transform us, He will lead us into the second phase. In this phase God wants to change the foundation stones on which our personalities have been built. He wants to go beyond the gentle, softening rain to the phase I call "open pit mining." Here God exposes our lies, our painful pasts, our strongholds and everything that hinders our relationship with Him and with others. This season is usually very painful and humbling. Many have told me that this was the most painful time of their lives. In His love and mercy, God allows us to see our bondages and pain so that we can begin our walk to freedom.

Kathy and I learned of these phases through personal experience. First, we enjoyed the gentle rain. Next came open pit mining. It was the most difficult thing we have ever experienced as God exposed all the lies and pain of our past and our marriage. It was 13 months of anguish, but at the end of it, we were transformed! Now we feel so free—it was worth every day of pain.

Over the past six years, Kathy has been transformed from a very conservative and inhibited Christian to an exuberant worshiper who directs our church's banner and flag department. She is now able to speak to groups about emotional recovery and worship. I have moved from being a general practitioner to being a mental health physician. I treat mood disorders during the week and do emotional recovery seminars on weekends.

Our church has quadrupled in size and is very healthy financially. Instead of worrying about losing the building, we now wonder how we can fit everyone in! Since the renewal, we thank God every day for His mercy and faithfulness in rescuing us from dry and lifeless Christianity. We will never go back.

**Note**

1. Guy Chevreau, *Catch the Fire* (New York: HarperCollins Publishers, 1994), p. 182.

# driven by whips or drawn by cords?

MARK STIBBE

*Rev. Dr. Mark Stibbe is a British theologian and vicar of St. Andrew's Chorleywood Anglican Church, just outside of London. He has written several books, including* From Orphans to Heirs: Celebrating Your Spiritual Adoption. *Here Mark tells of the remarkable encounter that set him free from the fear of rejection and brought him into a new intimacy with Father God.* —J. A.

One of Satan's battle plans is to do everything within his power to prevent us from enjoying the glorious freedom of the children of God. He does what he can to convince us that we have to earn the Father's acceptance through performance-oriented Christianity, rather than simply receive it as a free gift. Many believers get hooked by this deception; in time they become burned out rather than on fire.

To such individuals, the Father seems more and more remote. Christian ministry becomes an arduous duty rather than a constant joy, and the person becomes oppressed by a spirit of slavery and fear. Far from being led by the Holy Spirit into deeper and sweeter intimacy with Abba Father, he or she is driven by the flesh into greater and greater exhaustion. This is the way of the Pharisee, and its outward expression is always religious form without spiritual life or power. I speak from personal experience.

About five years ago I became acutely aware of a dryness in my walk with God and my service for Him. In my prayer life I no longer sensed God's intimate presence. He seemed far away and distant.

One Sunday evening in October 1995, I confessed this to my wife, Alie. She drew my attention to a Scripture that she had felt for several days was for me: "Jesus often withdrew to lonely places and prayed" (Luke 5:16, *NIV*). As we talked, I had a chilling sense of apprehension, a feeling of fear arising from something in the verse. At first I thought it might have been religious guilt at my failure to withdraw more often in order to pray for hours and hours on end. Then I realized it was something far deeper than that. I recognized that my real problem was a fear of being alone with the Father.

As we talked further, Alie suggested this fear might derive from the fact that when I was a baby, I was abandoned by my father. My twin sister and I were born in 1960, and we were very quickly placed in an orphanage in London, where we spent the first seven months of our lives. Dad left before we were even born, considering it too much responsibility to look after twins. This put a burden on my birth mother that she felt she could not carry. Mum, distraught and guilty, left us in care while Dad went off to enjoy life on his own.

My image of fathers was deeply marred by this experience. "Don't get too close to any father figure; he will end up abandoning you" was my motto. As Alie and I talked together that evening, we began to see there was a barrier in my heart that said to God "This close and no closer!" Jesus, however, came to show us that God is not a cruel, cosmic dictator but a passionate Father who longs for communion with us, His children. It became clear that I was not going to experience restored intimacy with my heavenly Father until I forgave my earthly father.

The Father's timing is always perfect. The very next day, I was due to leave for Toronto to visit the Airport Christian Fellowship for their annual Catch the Fire conference. I had heard about how the fire had fallen during the Randy Clark meetings in January 1994. I had also heard Bishop David Pytches describe how this renewal had impacted his own life during a day for leaders at Holy Trinity Brompton in July 1994. Even though I had received a number of invitations to visit Toronto, I had not felt it right to go until now.

Before we finished our discussion that Sunday night, Alie prayed for me. "Lord, if this is really You speaking and You want to heal this abandonment, then send Mark someone at the conference who will confirm this word and be used by You to bring healing and freedom, in Jesus' name."

The next day, I traveled to Toronto. When I went to my hotel room, I remember feeling very anxious about being alone and straightaway phoned Alie. I then resorted to the television for company and comfort. Finally I decided to turn to God! I offered up the prayer that Alie had encouraged me to pray.

On Tuesday, I went to the first main meeting of the conference. The worship was sweet, intimate and rich. The teaching issued from a heart on fire. Then came the ministry time. I ran forward to receive prayer, along with hundreds of others. I had already decided that I was going to use every possible opportunity to receive ministry. Even if the call was for barren women, I had made up my mind to go forward!

The next hour changed my whole life. A woman from the Toronto ministry team walked toward me. She had no idea who I was, and I had no idea who she was. But she pointed her finger at my heart and said, "Father, minister to the sense of abandonment in this man's heart." She then looked at me and asked, "Does this mean anything to you?" I said yes and shared how my birth parents had rejected my twin sister and me. She then prayed a very short prayer: "Father, make up the love deficit in this man's life." Simple as that! Nothing fancy. Nothing religious. Nothing long-winded, just "Father, make up the love deficit."

This prayer changed everything. Immediately I felt an upheaval in my stomach. I was not normally prone to show emotion, nor was I one to experience strong physical sensations in the presence of the Spirit. But out of my guts came a heartrending cry of grief and anger over my abandonment. I doubled up in pain and fell to the floor.

For the next few minutes (it felt like hours) I began to get in touch with an anger I had never felt before. I suddenly realized how bitter I was toward my birth parents for abandoning me, especially my dad, who never gave my mum, my sister and me a chance to make a go of it. I shouted out my grief and rage at him as I lay on the floor.

For what happened next you need a bit of background. About six months earlier, in the summer of 1995, I spoke at a conference in the United Kingdom. Afterwards, a lady sent me a letter. In it she shared that she had had a vision of me while I was preaching. She saw me speaking on the platform, but I had a ball and chain around my feet and a golden key in my right hand. She had no idea what the interpretation was but felt sure that I would know before long.

As I lay there, John Arnott stepped up to the microphone. He said, "I see many of you, especially pastors, with a ball and chain around your feet. But you have a golden key in your hands that will unlock your chains. Forgiveness is the golden key. So forgive those who have hurt and rejected you."

I knew exactly what I had to do. I shouted out, "I forgive you, Dad! I forgive you for abandoning and rejecting me. I release you right now from my bitterness. May the Lord bless you, wherever you are! May you come to know Him as your Savior!"

When I declared this, the peace of God came and saturated me. I was totally set free from the fear of rejection. I felt liberated from the slavery that had been oppressing me. In fact, I sensed a powerful deliverance going on in my life. As soon as that was complete, intimacy with my heavenly Father was restored. I staggered back to my hotel room a new man, no longer bound by the fear of abandonment! I had discovered for myself the wonderful truth of Psalm 27:10: "My father and mother walked out and left me, but *God took me in*" (*THE MESSAGE, emphasis added*).

# in love with the Father

If you were to ask me what it is that the Lord has been doing in Toronto since 1994, I would say that it is best summed up in John Wesley's phrase "the loving Spirit of adoption." My perspective is this: In January 1994, the Father opened up a well in Toronto. Out of that well has flowed the grace that enables people to fall in love with the Father.

I am well aware that many people have questions about what has been going on in Toronto. Our church, St. Andrew's Chorleywood, was radically impacted by this move of God. Yet there are still one or two members of St. Andrew's who take issue with me for writing and teaching in favor of Toronto. Their doubts mainly center around the issue of dramatic manifestations. Others have the same reservations. However, on pressing them, one often discovers that they have never been to Toronto or investigated it properly. I am in favor of a theological debate about what the British media call the Toronto Blessing, but I have to say that such hearsay critiques don't really help.

I believe that many believers are driven by whips rather than led by cords of love into radical service and genuine obedience.

What I see in Toronto is an astonishing outpouring of the Father's love, driving out fear and breaking off chains. It has truly been a place where orphans have become heirs and slaves have become sons. At the core of this move of God is *His amazing grace!*

I am also convinced that one day the history books will point to the significance of the Father's Blessing as the precursor to authentic revival in the Western world. Before the Great Awakening in eighteenth-century England, John Wesley was deeply touched by the Holy Spirit. His heart was strangely warmed as he fell passionately in love with his heavenly Father. Later he wrote of this experience as the work of "the loving Spirit of adoption." Wesley had come to that place described by the apostle Paul: "For you did not receive a spirit that makes you a slave again to fear, but you received the Spirit of sonship. And by him we cry, 'Abba, Father.' The Spirit himself testifies with our spirit that we are God's children" (Rom. 8:15,16, *NIV*). This moment marked the beginning of the great national revival that followed. Indeed, I know of few wide-scale revivals that have not been preceded by personal renewal of this kind.

Literally millions of Christian leaders, evangelists, missionaries, pastors and other professional church workers have been deeply impacted by what has flowed out of the well in Toronto. People from all over the world have learned once again to walk in the love of God, and have gone back to their ministries revived by the Holy Spirit and with a new passion for the lost. Not only are they walking in the love of God, but now they are more determined than ever to give it away to those who do not know Christ.

If you have not been to Toronto, let me say, "The well is still open. There is still time!" You will not regret going. The Father's invitation still stands: "Come, all you who are thirsty, come to the waters" (Isa. 55:1, *NIV*).

# God's appointed time

## BRENDA KILPATRICK

*I recall a very excited woman telling me that similar things had broken out in her church in Pensacola, Florida, as were taking place in Toronto. Little did we realize what a tremendous outpouring was to take place in Pensacola where Brenda serves alongside her husband, John, who is senior pastor of the Brownsville Assembly of God Church. Brenda is a contributor to the* Women of Destiny *Bible and is on the editorial board of* Spirit-Led Woman *magazine. The Kilpatricks have become dear friends. —J. A.*

When I was 18 years old and away from God, my mother had a dream from the Lord. He told her that if I would come to Him, I would eventually marry a minister who had great wisdom, and I would be happier than I had ever been. Although I forgot about the promise of marrying a preacher, I did give my heart to the Lord and started going to church. I began attending Riverview Assembly of God, where I eventually met and fell in love with a handsome young man. For 31 years now, that man has been a gift from the Lord to me.

John and I went away to Bible college for two years. Our funds were low when we found that we were expecting our first child. I realized that a diet of eggs, oranges and grapefruit would not provide the nourishment the baby inside me needed. We left college and went back to Georgia.

When our son Scott was nine months old, we accepted our first pastorate in Vidalia, Georgia. I was brand new in ministry and did not really know what was expected of me. Worse yet, I had no mentor. I wanted to please everyone and be a good pastor's wife. I tried so hard to fulfill all the demands of the ministry. I was hurting and had no one to talk to about my new role.

At times, feelings of unworthiness would come over me. I would cry to the Lord, "Why do I feel this way?" I felt as though I had done something wrong and had offended God. I listened, but the Lord was silent. I never stopped reading the Bible, and I would repent, confess and stand on the Word the best way I knew how. I was discouraged and had given up on myself, but I never let go of the hope I had in the Lord. Romans 5:5 *(KJV)* says, "Hope maketh not ashamed." Again, in Isaiah 49:23 *(KJV)*, "They shall not be ashamed that wait for me." I tried to do what was right but felt that I failed to measure up to my own expectations. My righteousness was as filthy rags. I was like a car that needed an oil change. God wanted to purify me and give me fresh oil. Eventually, there would come a season of change.

## waiting for God's appointed time

Many of us have experienced seasons of drought. Although we have been praying for rain, there is no rain cloud in sight. It is during these times that we must remain faithful and keep seeking His face.

In 1994, my pastor husband and I found ourselves in God's waiting room. While we fervently prayed for revival in our church, we had serious family needs. My mother-in-law was terminally ill with cancer. She was being cared for in a nursing home where I would go to see her every day. During this time, my husband heard that there was a move of God in Toronto. He encouraged me to go check it out and he would take over the care of Mom. I agreed, and in February 1995, my friend Shirl and

I flew to Toronto for a few days to see what God was doing. I didn't know what to expect, but I had heard God was in the house and I wanted more of Him.

The worship at the Toronto Airport Christian Fellowship was different from the Pentecostal style I was used to. The music was great and banners were waving as teenagers jumped and adults danced before the Lord. I knew this was God! During my first evening service there, I became very sleepy and felt I must be weary from the traveling. Later, I learned that what I thought was tiredness was in fact the *kabod* of the Lord, the weightiness of His presence. My friend and I wanted to be fresh to receive from the Lord the next day, so we did not stay until the end of the service for prayer.

We returned the next evening and again enjoyed the worship time. But the visiting minister's message didn't grab me. I said to the Lord, "If You are in this place, You had better come to me in the prayer line because I do not feel a thing!" We went and stood on the marked line and waited for God. A young lady came up to me and asked, "What do you need from the Lord?" I said, "I am a pastor's wife and I am here for a refreshing." She started to pray but never touched me. Immediately, I felt an intense heat on the top of my head that stopped at my neck. My toes went up, and I braced myself because I was not into courtesy falls; I wanted it to be God. Then I found myself on the floor! My friend said I lay on the floor for 45 minutes. That was a miracle in itself as I had previously had back trouble. The Lord completely healed me that night, and I have had no back problems since.

When I tried to get up, I couldn't—I was drunk in the Spirit! This was a whole new experience for me. As I sat there on the floor, I felt so silly! I looked around me and noticed a slightly overweight woman to my left, whose abdomen quivered like Jell-O when she wasn't groaning. I watched, and in my spirit

I knew God was healing her physically. A younger woman in her 20s was screaming "No! No!" I sensed that she had been violated as a child and that Jesus was setting her free. All around me I heard laughter. I also saw a man whose hands were trembling and shaking with such force that I was amazed. Nothing I saw or experienced that night offended me. I knew that God was doing in one hour what no doctor or psychiatrist could ever do. Shirl helped me up off the floor and back to our hotel room. We flew home the next day, not really knowing what God had done for me or what He had in store in the future.

The next Sunday morning, my husband wanted us to share about our trip to Toronto. Shirl and I had agreed beforehand not to mention anything about the physical manifestations we had observed. We wanted a sovereign move of God, in whatever fashion He chose. We shared how 3,000 people had come to Toronto from all over the world, with great expectation for healing and deliverance, and they were not disappointed! My husband encouraged the people to praise and thank the Lord for the soon-coming revival. After all, the Brownsville congregation had been seeking God for two and a half years, calling out around the prayer banners for a move of His Spirit.

John asked everyone to be seated and began his message. A woman in our congregation, named Georgia, who had been a barmaid prior to her salvation just one year earlier, remained standing while my husband continued to preach. She stood for 45 minutes, eyes closed and hands shaking, just like the man in Toronto! Later I found out that near where Georgia was standing, a member of the praise team had fallen to the floor under the power of the Holy Spirit. Then a man who had observed a horrible event at the age of eight and had been unable to cry since then, began to weep. I was so excited that I wrote the Holy Spirit a note: "Oh, Holy Spirit, You are here just like You are in

Toronto. Make our congregation as hungry for You as Georgia is. Oh, please send revival to us!"

One week later, I realized that I had experienced much more than just being drunk in the Spirit—I had been set free. Truly my "due season"—God's appointed time for me—had come. You see, I had strongholds in my life that I was dealing with, such as past hurts, a false image of myself, and feelings of unworthiness, guilt and shame. I even felt that my husband could have accomplished more in the ministry if he had chosen another wife! I had been believing the lies of the devil!

## saturated with His presence

When I came back from Toronto, I began to have an intimacy with the Lord that I never knew existed. I love John Kilpatrick, but this love I had for the Lord was different. This relationship was so deep and satisfying in my spirit. The Lord would awaken me in the morning as in previous times, but now it was different. There was an excitement and anticipation over meeting with Him. On many occasions I would wake up in the morning, go to my den and kneel down in front of my recliner. I would lay my head down as if it were in my Father's lap. Then I would say, "Father, here I am," and immediately His presence would come over me. It seemed as if I were a teabag in a teapot, enveloped by the warm water of God's presence. He was saturating me in His glory.

Every day I would spend hours before the Lord. I had prayed for years that the Lord would touch me and change my heart. I wanted to be pure and to please Him. Then when the Lord touched me, no words could be spoken; there were only tears of gratitude and deep love for Him. I felt waves of glory come over me. At times it was so intense that I recall saying to the Lord, "If

You don't stop, I'll die right here!" He had truly quieted me in His love (see Zeph. 3:17, *NKJV*).

Housework became less of a priority as I spent more time in the Lord's presence. One day I was in the laundry room, putting clothes in the washer, and I asked the Lord, "Do You know how much I loved You and served You when I did not feel You? And now do You know how much more I love You since I can feel You all the time?" You see, praying had become easy: upon kneeling, immediately I would feel His presence. The Bible became alive to me. I experienced a new level of worship and I began to enjoy the freedom of dancing before the Lord in our home. My husband would come home and see me dancing, and this began to increase his spiritual hunger. I had four wonderful months of intimacy with the Lord before revival broke out at Brownsville. It was His rest I had entered into!

We continued to pray for revival on Sunday evenings; the women had an additional prayer meeting on Thursday mornings. One Thursday, I left the sanctuary to go to the bathroom, where I saw two friends with whom I wanted to share a Scripture the Lord had given me. I asked them to come into the pastors' lounge. As I began to read, I felt waves of glory come on my head. I bowed my head and said, "Oh, I feel the Lord!" I was captured by His presence and didn't move for the next two hours! I could not speak, although I heard the ladies talking. Shirl was there, and she tried to explain to them how God had touched me.

A little later, my husband came in and asked, "What is wrong with my wife?" The ladies explained that I had been talking about the Lord and now I had been in this position for a long time. Then they excused themselves and went to pick up their children from school.

My husband sat down on the couch and said, "Are you all right? Do you think you could come out of this? We need to leave now because I have a board meeting tonight." I tried to open my eyes but couldn't. He began to rub my back, legs and arms, hoping to increase my blood circulation. Then he exclaimed, "Well, this must be the Lord!" All of a sudden I began to laugh. I saw a vision of a donkey with its mouth wide open, laughing, and that donkey was me! This laughter was all new to me; it sure wasn't very ladylike! It was gut-wrenching laughter that came between fits of weeping.

John finally managed to help me to the car and get me home. We changed clothes and went out to eat at a local cafeteria. As we sat in the dining area, eating our meal, my husband said, "You know, Brenda, if this happened to anyone else, I wouldn't believe it. But because I know you and I know your life, I know God is going to send revival to our church!" And with that, my husband began to weep! I laughed, knowing that he would never do anything like this in public. It was wonderful to see God touching him.

Not only was my husband hungry for God, but the church staff also began to hunger for more of the Lord. Most of them planned a trip to Toronto and were mightily touched by the Lord there. John tried to go with them, but he took ill and was unable to travel.

On Father's Day, June 18, 1995, we experienced a visitation from our heavenly Father. In that first morning service, my husband declared, "Folks, this is it! Get in—this is what we have been praying for!" Then, with no one touching him, he fell to the platform in the Spirit, where he remained for four hours! God kissed John and said, "Now, rest!"

It was around four o'clock in the afternoon when John got up off the floor and our youngest son, John Michael, helped him to the car. He sent John Michael back for me because we would be returning for the six o'clock service. I told our son, "Tell your dad I don't mean to be disrespectful, but we've prayed for two and a half years for God to show up. I am not about to leave, just in case He doesn't come back tonight!"

He did come back, and our church was forever changed. Today, five years later, over 3.5 million people have come from all over the world for more of the Lord. Over 134,000 people have been saved. Many backsliders have come home; others have been healed and delivered. Revival is awesome! Being able to witness souls coming to the Lord and seeing their lives so miraculously transformed is wonderful. The testimonies that are shared when these precious people get into the baptismal pool are incredible!

Now I truly know what church should be like. This is harvest time, the greatest ingathering the earth has ever seen. The Brownsville Outpouring is one small aspect of what God is going to do in the earth—only a prototype of what God wants to release into all the churches. We must have His presence if this harvest is to continue.

Moses completed every requirement for the design and construction of the Tabernacle, but what would it all have amounted to without the glory of God's presence inhabiting the holy of holies?

# touched by God

Revival will change your church and your family! John continues to give leadership to our church but has also been given a burden for pastors throughout the country. God has placed a special anointing on him as he encourages and ministers to them. The Lord has taken from me the timidity that kept me away from crowds; now I actually enjoy being able to share with ladies what God has done for me. And God has tremendously impacted our two sons and their wives. Having experienced the Lord's glory, our family will never be same. These five years of revival have changed our purpose and destiny forever! My prayer is that you also will be transformed as God touches you with His glory. And then, may the Lord of the harvest raise up laborers for His work.

# floored in toronto

## STEPHEN STRANG

*Stephen Strang is the founder and president of Strang Communications— a publisher of books and periodicals, including Charisma magazine, through which Steve has served the Body of Christ for over 25 years. Subsequent to Charisma doing several news articles on TACF, Steve came to see for himself what was happening. I remember meeting and chatting with him, which eventually led to his (Creation House) publishing my book The Father's Blessing. At one particular meeting, Carol had begun praying for Steve and soaking him in the presence of the Holy Spirit. About 20 minutes later, he was on the floor, under the power of God. He tells of the impact. (The first part of this story first appeared in Charisma magazine in February 1995.) —J.A.*

I didn't pay much attention to the so-called Toronto Blessing until I began to hear of its impact in England. Undoubtedly, some of the manifestations that have been reported with this move are strange. But because I am personally acquainted with some of the British leaders who have been affected, I knew I needed to check it out.

In November 1994, my wife and I visited the Airport Christian Fellowship in Toronto, the scene of the meetings that had been drawing tens of thousands of international visitors for more than a year. Over a period of three days I saw things I'd never seen before in a church service.

One woman thrashed around on the floor as if she were in labor. A young man flailed his arms, moving them like the sails of a windmill. Several people acted as if they were hit by bolts of electricity.

Despite these and other unusual manifestations, however, I could see that people were being touched by God in a deep way. As I met with some of them later, they exhibited a pure devotion to God—an abandonment in the Spirit—that went far beyond what I usually encounter in Christians (and what I often exhibit in my own life).

The first meeting in Toronto didn't do much for me. The praise and worship were good, but I had trouble getting used to my surroundings. On the second night I enjoyed the service more but still didn't experience anything unusual.

The next day we met with John Arnott and his wife, Carol. As we talked about what God was doing in Toronto and my own guarded reaction to the phenomenon, Arnott joked that he had a special designation for people like me: HTR—hard to receive.

At that night's service, I determined I wanted whatever God had for me, but I wasn't going to do anything just because others were. So when everyone else seemed to be falling on the floor, I was left standing.

After the service, I asked Carol Arnott to pray for me. She and a group of others surrounded me and prayed for what must have been 20 minutes. At that point, I felt totally overcome by God's presence and fell backward onto the floor—only the second time in my life that such a thing had happened to me.

"More. Give him more, Lord," they continued to pray. One lady prophesied. Then they left me on the floor alone for about an hour.

I didn't roar, nor did I shake. I don't think I moved a muscle. I was totally conscious the entire time. Yet in the process I was aware that the Lord was doing a deep work in my heart.

# current reflections

It is interesting to read my words nearly six years later and see that some of the concerns I had have not actually been realized. For example, I wondered if shaking would become a sign of spirituality.

I was also reminded that my experience of falling at the service in Toronto was only the second time that it had happened to me. It certainly has happened a lot of times since then. Undoubtedly the Lord did something in my life to soften me up. I am not nearly so hard to receive now.

After that initial trip to Toronto, I have been there several more times and have done several television interviews, which we ran on our *Charisma Now* television program on TBN. In one service I remember John called me forward and asked me to share a few words. Several people gathered around my wife and me. My wife went onto the floor, but I stood there for more than half an hour thinking, *If God wants me to go down, He's going to have to make me go down.* Finally, after about half an hour, everyone gave up. Meanwhile, the service had gone on and I just slipped quietly back to my seat.

The next time I went to Toronto and was invited up to greet the audience, I thought to myself that there was no way I was going to go down if they prayed for me. Boy, was I wrong. Immediately I was on the floor. But this time I could not get up. The service went on while I laid there on the platform. After a while I was aware that I couldn't move a muscle. I had heard of people giving testimony of this phenomenon but had always been a little doubtful.

You have to understand that I'm the kind of person who likes to have enough control of my own muscles that I can move from point A to point B when I want to do so. This time I was just absolutely helpless.

The interesting thing, as I reflect upon it and comment on it several years later, is that the Lord really did do something in my heart as I was lying there on the floor. Why do I share this with you? I do it partly to show that even though I am known as a journalist and observer of the Body of Christ, I do not have all the answers. I guess it is my way to be vulnerable and to let you know that God is working in me too. It is also to let you know that the ministry of John and Carol Arnott has impacted me. What has happened at Toronto has motivated me to seek out other locations that are experiencing revival, which means that since I first visited Toronto I have also visited Holy Trinity Brompton and Sunderland, England; Buenos Aires, Argentina; and, of course, Brownesville Assembly, Pensacola, Florida. God has used the revival fires in one place to inspire others.

The important thing to focus on, however, is not the revival hot spots, as I call them, but the revival in our own hearts. All of us need to ask ourselves, Are we open to the Holy Spirit? Are we living lives pleasing to God? Are we overcoming the attacks of the enemy and changing our world?

# undeniable power of the Holy Spirit

## BILL PRANKARD

*Bill Prankard is a well-known, Canadian-based evangelist who has brought much healing and blessing to our nation. He received a powerful touch of the Holy Spirit at a Kathryn Kuhlman meeting in Pittsburgh in 1972. Since then, he has poured out his life for God in a healing and evangelistic ministry. Additionally, he has been ministering for 25 years to the Inuit (Eskimo) people. But by the '90s, Bill was very dry like the rest of us. I remember meeting him in our overflow room at Derry and Dixie Roads Auditorium. While he stood on the prayer lines like all the others, God came and touched him powerfully. We have since struck up a close friendship, and Bill and Gwen, his wife, have been frequent ministers at our Toronto meetings. —J. A.*

My encounter with the Holy Spirit has been an ever-increasing journey of letting Him nudge, or sometimes jolt, me out of my comfort zone. I do not take His anointing for granted. Every day I must walk in relationship with Him—relying on Him, depending on His grace. His anointing has taken me around the world, ministering healing power to millions and sharing the reality of Jesus' love and miracle-working power. Some of the most recent anointing has happened at Toronto Airport Christian Fellowship. But the beginning of the story is 1970—six years into my Pentecostal pastoral ministry. At that time, I came into genuine relationship with the Holy Spirit.

I had begun serving as pastor of a little Pentecostal church in Beachburg, Ontario, a tiny village in Canada's Ottawa Valley. I thought I'd received everything God had to offer—I was forgiven, healed, filled with the Holy Spirit and called to preach. In my mind, I'd earned all the "badges"!

Two years later there was little to show for all my efforts. The congregation of 50 faithful souls endured my arrogance and cliché-filled sermons. My doctrine on the Holy Spirit was correct. But I didn't know just how powerless my ministry was until a memorable Friday just before Easter in 1972, when I was invited to accompany a busload of people on a trip to Pittsburgh, Pennsylvania, where Kathryn Kuhlman was conducting weekly miracle services.

I'd heard mixed opinions about Miss Kuhlman's ministry, which made me hesitant to go, but I eventually accepted the invitation. The 12-hour journey was surprisingly pleasant as the passengers sang and fellowshiped and shared their expectations. Many had come with incurable conditions, ailments and physical limitations.

At dawn our group joined hundreds of fellow worshipers as they waited on the steps of the First Presbyterian Church in Pittsburgh and quietly sang and prayed. When the doors opened around 8:00 A.M., we jostled and squeezed our way into the auditorium. I found a seat about three-quarters of the way back. A few minutes later the service began.

As the piano and organ created a worshipful atmosphere, a willowy figure dressed in a flowing white gown came almost floating across the stage. A strategically placed fan gently blew the billowing skirt, while a spotlight followed her every move. In a husky, deliberate tone, Miss Kuhlman whispered, "Jee-sus, don't let them see me; let them see You." In my critical state, I muttered to myself, "If you don't want them to see you, turn off the spotlight and wear a black dress!" I definitely had an attitude! But as the service progressed, I realized I was hardly conscious of Miss Kuhlman. I sensed only an overwhelming presence of God.

Miss Kuhlman began praying for people, and as she moved toward them, sometimes gently touching them, they fell to the floor. I had never seen a sight like this in my life! One person after another was overcome with God's power and presence as they received healing, blessing and deliverance.

At that moment I felt a finger press into my chest and knew it was supernatural. In my spirit I heard the Holy Spirit say, "Yes, this *is* My power, and you have had a form of godliness and denied My power!"

I wept uncontrollably as the reality of my pitiful spiritual state hit me full force. In that moment I understood that I didn't have a relationship with the Holy Spirit; I had simply encountered Him from time to time. For years I had taught He is a person, not a force—a doctrine I believed wholeheartedly. Yet I'd been practicing the doctrine, rather than developing a relationship with Him. I repented through floods of tears.

I witnessed more miracles in that one service than I'd seen in my entire life. As we boarded the bus to begin the long journey home, my heart was filled to overflowing.

Everyone on the bus was praising God for all they had seen and heard; but as we visited, we discovered that no one on the bus had received a healing. Moments later I heard an inner voice say, "I'm healing someone"; and He described the condition. I had never heard the Holy Spirit's voice in this way before. I didn't know what to do with this knowledge. As I pondered, someone came up behind me. "This lady was just healed!" she declared. It was exactly as the Lord had revealed to me. Soon, one after another began shouting, "I've just been healed!" and they stood and testified to God's healing power. As I laid my hands on them to pray, they fell to the floor, overcome by the Holy Spirit's presence. I was stunned.

When we returned to Beachburg, I didn't know how to explain to my wife or to anyone else what I'd experienced. I only knew I'd never be the same.

The following Sunday, in my overwhelmed state, I approached my church's platform and headed toward a chair where I usually knelt momentarily in a supposedly pious act of prayer before the beginning of the service. In all honesty, prayer was not my main focus. Normally I would be thinking, *I hope they don't see the holes in the soles of my shoes* and *I wonder if I've knelt long enough to give the right impression.*

But this day, as I approached the chair, I suddenly stopped, knowing I could no longer carry on this charade. I turned and headed for the pulpit. Again the Holy Spirit arrested me and said, "I've been waiting for you to step out of the way for a long time."

My congregation must have thought I was having a breakdown as they watched my halting actions. Through tears I poured out my heart as I recounted what God had done in my life, and I vowed that, with His help, I would never again limit the Holy Spirit.

At the conclusion of the service, several parishioners came to me and declared, "Pastor, as you spoke this morning, God healed my body!" I had done nothing to precipitate such a reaction. The Holy Spirit had simply taken control.

After the service I retreated to my study, where I stayed on my face before God. Lost in His presence, time flew by, and I suddenly realized it was time for the evening service. As I headed out the door into the lobby, I was amazed at the sight before me. The church was packed to capacity!

That was the first miracle service I ever conducted. I was as amazed as anyone else when people streamed forward to testify of God's healing touch in their bodies. When I gave an altar call for salvation, at least half the congregation responded. It was nothing I was doing—it was simply the Holy Spirit taking control.

From then on, week after week, the crowds grew until I had to put a sound system out on the church lawn to allow those who could not get inside, the opportunity to at least hear the service. Busloads from neighboring cities and towns began arriving to participate in the outpouring.

The miracles continued and the region was profoundly impacted.

Eventually I sensed the Holy Spirit was urging me to go into full-time evangelistic ministry. We moved our headquarters to the nation's capital, Ottawa, and began conducting weekly miracle services. A thousand people gathered every week, bringing the sick, the broken and the lost. And God was faithful, touching their lives and making them whole. Out of those meetings, a thriving church developed and continues today.

I had begun a pursuit for relationship with Holy Spirit, not just an encounter.

For nearly 25 years, I ministered in this new understanding of anointing. I was comfortable in this relationship and assumed that what had happened in Ottawa would be my mode of ministry forever. But in 1994, a visit to the Toronto Airport Chirstian Fellowship stretched me even further.

I remember the first renewal service I attended at the TACF. The worship team was dressed in wrinkled T-shirts and cutoff jeans. The host was *talking* instead of preaching. This apparently casual approach to God was at first somewhat disconcerting. But when my spirit got beyond the cultural differences, I experienced the overpowering sense of God's presence. Then, when the invitation was given to receive personal ministry, I was surprised to see that the ministry team did not consist of *professionals* but *laypeople* whom the Spirit was using to pour blessing into their peers.

Although, as a Pentecostal, I preached about the authority of the believer and encouraged Christians to minister to others, in practice most churches I had observed still left personal ministry to the pastoral staff. It was unusual for me to see this church releasing its people to reach out to one another. In my own services as a healing evangelist, it had seldom occurred to me to ask believers to lay hands on each other to receive miracles. This new approach was definitely out of my comfort zone.

Something about God's tangible presence, however, made me want to return. A few months later when I was in Toronto again, I slipped over to an afternoon session already in progress where prayer was being offered to pastors and ministry leaders.

I stood watching as lines of men and women opened their lives to the Holy Spirit and began receiving. Several fell to the floor and lay there for extended periods of time. Others sat, stood or knelt as the river of God flowed through their lives. Some were crying; others wept; and still others reacted with shaking, groaning and various other unusual movements. Through it all, I recognized that God was doing a significant work in many of them.

A friend who had attended several of these meetings came over to me and said, "If you want prayer you have to stand on a red line." I saw several lines created from red duct tape placed strategically across the altar area at the front of the auditorium, along the sides and throughout a large open area at the back.

*A little unorthodox,* I mused, but I obediently made my way to the nearest red line.

Momentarily, a big man with a friendly face sauntered by. "You're Bill Prankard, aren't you?" he said. By his tone I knew he recognized me from somewhere. Later I learned the friendly face belonged to John Arnott.

"Bless him, Lord," John prayed as he gently placed his hand on my head. I sensed the presence of God and fell to the floor, assisted by a readily available catcher. In a few moments I stood to my feet.

John returned and laid his hand on me again, and once again I fell down. Within minutes I was back on my feet again.

John came back again, but this time called some of his ministry team members. "This is Bill Prankard," he informed them. "He needs more. Don't let him go until he's been soaked."

They began ministering to me and this time stayed with me as I lay prostrate for a lengthy period. During my time in God's presence, I realized just how much I'd missed by getting up before God was finished. Holy Spirit had stretched me again and I decided to let Him keep doing it.

That significant experience led to a special bond of friendship between John Arnott and me. Soon John invited me to speak at a midweek renewal service. I was awed by the presence of God and the hunger of people who had come from all over the world to receive the Father's Blessing. Subsequent visits were just as meaningful, and within a few months I committed to conduct the renewal meetings on a regular basis. Every time I minister at the Toronto Airport Christian Fellowship, I receive more than I give out. The renewing, restoring, refreshing presence of God has added a new dimension to my ministry.

God does not want us to stay in our comfort zones. He wants us to seek more of Him on every level. I no longer refer to the third Person of the Trinity as "the" Holy Spirit. He is Holy Spirit, my friend, my companion, my source of anointing. He is not simply a power, a force or a doctrine. He is fully God, as much as our heavenly Father and Jesus are God. The more I seek

Him, the greater my hunger for Him grows. I have seen many outstanding miracles, but there is so much more! Keep coming, Holy Spirit!

# fishes find the river!

## MELINDA FISH

---

*Melinda Fish is a Christian author now working on her sixth book,* Keep Coming, Holy Spirit: Cherishing Revival. *She is also the editor of our TACF magazine* Spread the Fire. *Melinda is one of our favorite people on Earth. I love her story of how God saw the deep hunger in her heart and, following a long desert experience, satisfied that hunger. This Fish loves the river: she has come to soak in Toronto over 35 times! —J. A.*

## the promise and the pain

It was 2:30 A.M. I had been awake only a few minutes, but the tears were already coming. I buried my head in the pillow and tried to hide my crying from my husband. There were days when it didn't bother me, but sometimes the pain of it was just too much. After 18 years of struggle, the church Bill and I pastored in Trafford, Pennsylvania, had a regular attendance of only 60 people. Church planting had not been easy.

In 1976, we arrived in Pittsburgh to take the pastorate of a struggling denominational church in an inner-city neighborhood. Before leaving Dallas to head north, we attended a series of meetings where Ed Miller was speaking. He was the missionary in whose church the Argentinean Revival had reportedly begun more than three decades earlier.

In one of those meetings, Bill saw a vision of a snowcap melting on a mountaintop. As he watched, rivulets of water began to form, flowing down the mountainside and accumulating behind a dam. Finally, the pressure of the snowmelt created a crack in the dam's wall. Suddenly the wall broke, sending a flood of water into the valley below. The scene changed, and Bill saw a tiny weather-beaten church in the middle of a desert. A trickle of water began to flow from under the doorway of the building. The flow continued until the desert was saturated with water. Then vegetation sprang up around the ever-widening river, turning the desert into a lush valley.

A few weeks after we arrived in Pittsburgh, one of our former pastors paid us a visit and gave us the Scripture we clung to for the next 18 years. "Do not call to mind the former things, or ponder things of the past. Behold, I will do something new. Now it will spring forth; will you not be aware of it? I will even make a roadway in the wilderness, rivers in the desert" (Isa. 43:18,19).

From that time on, we tried to believe that every passing year would be the time when the river would spring forth. We struggled through inner-city ministry, riding the roller coaster of hope and disappointment as people would come, stay for a while, then grow discouraged and leave. In 1985, we relocated the church to the suburbs, hoping that the move would bring the long-awaited vision to pass. It didn't. Instead, more people left. By then, around 40 people turned out for Sunday morning meetings.

From time to time, there were signs of encouragement. Guest ministers who came our way would prophesy about events to come. They would stop the flow of their sermons and begin to prophesy that one day we would see a river and something called the Blessing.

The years slipped by. Our children grew up and we began to wonder if we had somehow missed God. Why were we having such a struggle? The methods that seemed to work so easily for others never worked in our church, at least not for very long. We had tried everything we knew: fasting, prayer, church growth seminars, evangelism efforts, outreaches, sowing into missions. Enthusiasm would last a few weeks and then fizzle into business as usual. What we really longed for was a true revival like we had seen before we left Dallas, but it never came.

The pain of barrenness taught us some powerful lessons about compassion. The struggles we faced exposed raw human needs, and I began to write about them. By 1993 I had published five books and was receiving mail from people all over the country who could identify with our battles. Even though the Lord blessed me this way, I longed to see something more—the river that God had promised. But I was growing weary of waiting.

One night in 1993, I lay awake praying, "O God, I don't know what's wrong! Maybe we're doing something that is grieving the Holy Spirit, or maybe we are in the wrong place. Maybe it's the wrong time; but if You'll just open a door, I promise You we'll leave."

At 7:30 the next morning, our telephone rang. It was Sheila Johnson-Hunt, a pastor's wife from another church across town. I hadn't talked to Sheila in quite a while. Without saying hello she blurted, "You're in the right place. And this is the right time! Now, Lord, may I please go to sleep?" Sheila had been awake since 2:30 A.M. with this message practically pounding in her head. God had directly spoken a word to her for me! It was the first clue in a long time that the Lord was even listening to my prayers.

But the year passed and nothing seemed to happen. In the spring of 1994, I had major surgery and began to immediately suffer hormone shock. For the first time in my life, I began to experience panic attacks. I would wake up suddenly in the middle of the night with my heart pounding and a sense of impending doom smothering me. Bill would hold me until I stopped shaking. I was beginning to know the face of mental torment and wondered if I would have to check into a hospital for treatment.

# something in the wind

During the summer of 1994, Bill and I began to hear about what was happening in Toronto. It wasn't good. People were laughing and making animal noises in the meetings in some church up there near the airport. I concluded that they were only being carried away emotionally. "Oh puh-lease," I said, "not something else scampering across the screen of the Body of Christ!"

Then in August, we received a letter from our friends George and Joanne Stockhowe of Virginia Beach, where George was rector of Church of the Messiah Episcopal. Their letter made me take a second look. "There are no stars up there, only nameless people. People are lining up from all over the world to get into the meetings." The Stockhowes had selected 30 friends from their Christmas card list to notify about their trip to Toronto. Joanne later told me that she had wavered as she held the stamp on her finger. She almost didn't paste it on our letter, thinking to herself, *The Fishes never go for things like this.* Thank God she sent it!

We received their letter during our annual week of prayer and fasting at the end of the summer. That Friday night we were to break the fast with a buffet dinner at the church. To my amazement, everyone was there. We ate together and then filed upstairs to have a time of sharing. One by one people began to tell how during the week they had realized how dry they were and that they needed more of the Lord. This was better than the usual awe-provoking testimonies that went something like, "Well, my cat was sick and now it's better."

Suddenly, the visitation presence of the Lord that I had felt so long ago in Dallas sank down and began to hover over the congregation. We froze in our seats. People looked at each other. "Do you feel that?" we all wondered. Then individuals lifted up their voices and just began to sing, not our charismatic worship songs, but hymns. This spontaneous hymn singing went on in our services for several weeks. The Holy Spirit was very present, as though He were hanging around, waiting for something.

In October, Bill and I made our first trip to England. There we visited Kevin and Pam Swadling (now the directors of Christ for the Nations, in the United Kingdom) and went with them to church on Sunday morning. That day they called the visitors forward for personal ministry. Members of the congregation began to lay hands on us and pray. One of the women began to prophesy, "You've been waiting on Me for years. Everything you've been waiting for is behind a curtain. And I'm about to part the curtain!"

I couldn't hear any more prophecies; I wanted some fulfillments. *Put it in the bag with all the others!* I thought, steeling myself against further disappointment. Even though something was happening at home, it was still not enough after 18 years of struggling.

A week later we visited friends in Spain. One night in a dream, I saw my husband and me entering a restaurant. Seated at a table nearby were a well-known healing evangelist and his wife. I went over to them and began to tell them how badly we needed revival. While I was talking to them, their countenances changed to that of two men. One of them interrupted me and said, "Have I not promised you times of refreshing from the Lord?" When the words left his mouth, I felt an overwhelming sense of the presence of God, stronger than I had felt in years of emotional numbness.

A few weeks later, during American Thanksgiving, Bill and I decided to take our 15-year-old son and two of our friends to Toronto. On the way up I wondered what I was getting into. The night before, a well-meaning woman in our church had handed us a letter, warning us of deceiving spirits in Toronto. I thought to myself, *I don't know much right now, but I'll know whether or not it's God if they are talking about Jesus.*

# arrival in toronto

We arrived in Toronto in time for the Wednesday afternoon pastors' meeting. As I looked around the room, I wondered at how people from Africa, Korea, Australia, Finland, the United Kingdom, and the United States could all wind up in a small church in a commercial plaza near the airport runway in Toronto, Canada. The meetings had never been formally advertised!

Theologian Guy Chevreau was describing how early revivals had seen powerful emotional manifestations, similar to what people were experiencing in Toronto, with the lingering effect of renewed love for Jesus. There was enough mention of Jesus in that meeting to make us feel safe about receiving prayer. As they cleared away the chairs and the ministry team began to pray for the pastors, everything we had heard about Toronto started happening around us. Pastors were all over the floor. Some were laughing; others, touched by an unseen presence, were crying out with an emotional intensity I had never seen before.

A few moments later, Guy Chevreau saw us standing there and came to pray for us. "What are your names?" he asked. "We're the Fishes and we're really dry," I replied. Guy gently laid hands on us and said, "Well then, let the river flow." Immediately the presence of the Holy Spirit began to seep into our dry souls.

His prophetic prayer was more than a sign to us. So while others were laughing, Bill and I wept.

The meeting the next night was in the larger auditorium where the church now meets. A wave of laughter swept over the crowd of more than two thousand people. I found myself laughing too. As the testimonies began, I was transfixed. A pastoral couple who had also been dry and discouraged had witnessed a wind of revival sweep into their congregation, changing people's lives. After they testified, ministry team members prayed for them. The woman fell to the floor and her feet began to do a drumroll on the carpet faster than would be naturally possible. Her socks began to slip off her feet. My son, wide-eyed with awe, leaned over and whispered, "Look, Mom! She's prophesying her socks off!"

The testimony of the next woman captured me. She said, "One year ago, my husband and I were chronic TV watchers. We didn't even want to go to church. . . ."

*Sounds familiar,* I thought. *I'm a pastor and I don't want to go either.* She continued, "But in January someone called one evening and said, 'Get down to the church! God's moving!' We did, and we've been back every night since. And tonight I'm more in love with Jesus than I have ever been in all my life!"

Under the power of God's presence, the woman was vibrating so much that her head was shaking. Every pastoral instinct in me wanted to grab her head and tell her to stop shaking, until I heard "in love with Jesus." When she said those words, it was as though a spear ran through my heart. I began to cry, "Oh, Lord, of all the things I've lost in these years of struggle, it's my first love for Jesus! I'll do anything to get it back!"

At the end of the service, we stood waiting for prayer. A ministry team member approached us, smiling. "May I pray for you?" he asked. "Certainly," we replied, trying not to appear too needy. Though I put on my best pastor's-wife smile, inside I was thinking,

*Well, take your best shot, because I never go down.* Ron Dick simply reached out two fingers and lifted up the prayer that brought heaven down after 18 years of waiting. He said, "Come, Holy Spirit!"

I felt a gentle pressure on my chest. Before this moment I had never fallen in response to prayer. I placed little value on the experience, having seen very little fruit from it. Now it was as though a gentle wind was pressing me backward. The man wasn't pushing us or intimidating us in any way. I now had a choice. I could either respond to God's presence and the way He wanted to touch me, or I could stiffen myself, resist and risk quenching the first powerful intrusion of God into my life in years. I fell backward onto the floor, completely surrounded by a sense of the love of God.

In my mind's eye, I could see the shadow of Jesus bending over me. He was laughing! In my head I could hear Him speaking, "Well now, you'll never be able to brag about not having been down under the power again, will you?" For over half an hour I felt too weak to get up. I didn't want to. The love of God was filling me for the first time in years.

# the river hits trafford!

We came home to Pittsburgh and called a meeting of the church. Bill explained to the congregation what had happened. To everyone's amazement, our son testified about how God had touched him. Not wanting to pressure anyone, Bill offered to begin praying for others at the next meeting.

In the following service, people began to trickle forward for prayer. The first person to receive prayer was Nancy Westerberg, our children's pastor. For three years she had been in a depression. Bill lightly touched her forehead and then put his hands behind his back so she would know that she wasn't being pushed.

Nancy fell to the floor and her feet began to do a drumroll on the carpet. Then her arms began to sway in the air. She jumped up, grabbed my hands and began to dance me all over the room! After she had worn me out, she went on to the next person. For weeks her feet danced, even in the middle of the night. Her depression left immediately and has not returned. As she lay in bed at night, she would touch her husband lying next to her. Burt had been scheduled for surgery to remove a large calcified cyst from his leg. His surgery was canceled!

Within weeks we saw five healings, confirmed by doctors and radiologists. Laughter broke out in our meetings, and business as usual came to a halt. We determined to throw open the door to allow God to move in every service and not confine Him to one night a week.

For over six years now, the Holy Spirit has shown up at every single service in a new dimension of His powerful presence. As we have simply stepped back and allowed the Holy Spirit to touch lives as He sees fit, we have seen the lost saved and an influx of hungry people from all over the tri-state area of southwestern Pennsylvania, West Virginia and Ohio. We believe God has told us to "keep the fire lit, because it will catch on all around." In our Friday night renewal service we freely give away the blessing for which we waited over 18 years. We have seen thousands pass through the doors of our church and find a renewed first-love passion for Jesus.

## taking the fire to prison

Two years into the renewal, we received a letter from a prison inmate in Virginia, about a five-hour drive from Pittsburgh. He had read a magazine article I had written about the river of

God's blessing and wanted more information. By this time I had written my fifth book, *The River Is Here*. The prisoner devoured it and asked for more. He sent us a piece of notebook paper with his handprint traced on the page. "We know you can't come to us," he wrote, "but we believe that if you would just have your team pray over this piece of paper, the Toronto Blessing will come to our prison."

A few weeks later, a team of 14 volunteers gave up a holiday weekend with their families to travel to another state and spread the fire to the Augusta Correctional Facility in Craigsville, Virginia. That weekend was the turning point for many of those men, as well as for us. Hardened criminals wept, and several fell under the power as hands were laid on them and they, too, were surrounded by the Father's love. Charlie, a black Muslim in prison for armed robbery, came to Jesus Christ. We have ministered there six times in the last four years, and we receive mail from them weekly. "I don't know what we would have done here," wrote one inmate, "if you hadn't come to share this with us." God has also opened doors to other prisons, where inmates have eagerly embraced the river of God's presence.

# the river still flowing!

It has been nearly seven years since God began moving on us. In the past two years, Bill and I have traveled to eight nations and from coast to coast in the United States, sharing about the powerful dimension of God's love that He is pouring out in our day. At this writing, our church has grown to 150 people. The adults, youth and children are all alive with a newfound passion for Jesus. Over 40 percent of the young people believe God is calling them to full-time Christian ministry! As we continue basking in the Father's love, doors keep opening to spread what we have received. The curse of barrenness has been broken as we simply soak in the river of God's presence. Life is seeping out the doors of our once weather-beaten church, and God's presence is turning the desert into a lush valley full of fruit and blessing. Don't be trying to tell me this isn't God! I've seen too much!

# shedding my pentecostal pride

## LINDELL COOLEY

*Lindell Cooley is music director of Brownsville Assembly of God in Pensacola, Florida and oversees a ministry called Music Ministry International. He has produced several CDs associated with the Brownsville Revival. I met this passionate worship leader on my first visit to the Brownsville Revival in the spring of 1996. I had heard so much about the wonderful move of God there and was heartily welcomed by the leaders. Here is Lindell's amazing testimony. —J. A.*

I recall 1994 as being one of the most difficult years of my life. I seemed to be in a continuous state of transition throughout that year. I was serving as an itinerant minister and having some success; God was blessing the ministry. But inside I felt empty and extremely hungry for something I couldn't put my finger on. I knew this hunger—this gnawing ache for more—had been placed there by the Lord, but I also had no idea how He was going to satisfy it.

Sometimes, I would hear stories about the Toronto Blessing but dismissed it as another charismatic happening like so many I had seen during my growing-up years. There was always something new to draw the attention of the Church for a short season which eventually would fade away.

The articles I read about John Arnott's church always listed both the pros and the cons of what had happened in the services; any criticisms I read only helped to fuel my suspicion that this was just another frivolous event. But as time went on, and people were still coming from all over the world, I knew this had to be more than just another one of the Church's tangents. This had to be God; He had to be doing something special to sustain meetings over such a length of time.

After many months of seeking the Lord and wondering which way to go, I received a call from John Kilpatrick. He and I were more or less acquaintances and I respected him for his solid preaching and teaching. He was a middle-of-the-road, conservative Assembly of God pastor serving in Pensacola, Florida.

He explained how he had just lost his music minister, who had moved to care for ailing parents. He had thought of calling me at least two or three times and had dismissed the idea. Something inside pushed him to finally complete the call. He told me, "I feel that God has directed me to call you and I believe you're supposed to be at Brownsville."

I knew I was in a season of change, but I wasn't sure that moving to Pensacola and becoming the worship leader at a mostly conservative church was the right destination. I told him I wasn't interested, but we kept in touch.

One day I talked with him and asked, "What do you think about what's going on in Toronto?"

He paused and said, "I don't know, Lindell, but my wife and a lady from our church are thinking of going. They're both women of prayer and solid in the Word of God, so I feel I can trust their opinions on the matter when they return. When they come back, we'll get the whole story."

John and I were so hungry to see God move, but our years in the ministry had taught us to be cautious and not embrace every whim of the Church. Every time we talked I was anxious to hear if there was any news from the expedition into the unknown. At the same time, my heart began to change toward the music ministry position at Brownsville. God had made it clear that He was calling me to Pensacola, so I called John and accepted the position.

During another conversation, John told me his wife had returned from Toronto and told him it was wonderful. He said, "I've been married to Brenda for all these years and she's not a strange woman, but God is moving on her in ways I've never seen. Quite frankly, it's making me jealous for the Lord."

He explained that he was so moved by the changes he had witnessed in his wife that he was releasing some of his staff to go to Toronto. He asked if I wanted to go. I eagerly accepted and decided to call my father to see if he wanted to make the journey with me. My father had been in ministry for over 25 years and comes from a conservative Pentecostal background. I knew he would have a balanced perspective.

Two months later—a week before I was supposed to move to Brownsville—my father and I were on our way to Toronto. By this time we had heard the stories of the laughing, falling down and other manifestations. As proven Pentecostals, both my father and I had seen these spiritual reactions through the years, but the fact that they were occurring in a non-Pentecostal church birthed outside the Bible Belt was rather humbling. It upset my spiritual pride.

After Dad and I checked into the hotel room, we prepared to attend our first service. It was snowing outside and, fortunately, it wasn't long before they moved the line to the inside of the warehouselike building where we met our new friends from Brownsville. When the service started, I discovered that the Arnotts were out of town ministering and the worship band was traveling too. There was a preacher from California, and a lady playing the guitar led worship.

The whole approach to the church service at Toronto was much more laid-back than I was used to. The musician inside of me began picking apart the service: the sound wasn't great; the overhead projectors were hard to read; the music was the opposite of what I enjoyed. I was used to a more upbeat gospel presentation of music. I now realize that what I used to call worship—for the most part—was Christian entertainment.

It wasn't long into the sermon before I realized it was a very basic, simple gospel message. I had become used to preaching that was characterized by great oratory skill and length. This sermon was clearly a meat-and-potatoes message.

At the end of the service, the minister stood up and gave an invitation to receive prayer. People rushed forward until the front was filled. The minister said, "If there isn't any room at the front, then you can go to the back of the building where you will find pieces of duct tape on the floor. Please line up behind the duct tape and wait for someone to pray with you."

I thought, *Oh great. I don't get to go to the front where it's really happening. I get put in the back of the building under harsh fluorescent lighting, where the music is barely intelligible. That's where I'm supposed to receive what God is sending?* But I had traveled a long way to see this, so I obeyed.

My toes were touching the worn tape line and my cynicism ran extremely high. I felt silly. I finally put my hands in the air and said, "Okay, God, I'm here. I don't see anything and I don't feel anything. But I suppose You are here. And my hunger for You is stronger than my cynicism."

Finally, a little guy wearing Hush Puppies shoes and with a soft voice began praying for me. He wasn't even praying like I was used to being prayed for. He said, "Fill him with more of Jesus; wash over my brother's spirit and touch him with Your glory." He prayed for a long time but nothing happened. I was getting very frustrated.

Finally, he said, "You need to get yourself in a posture to receive. You've got your hands up like you're bringing a jet in for a landing. You need to put your palms up in a receiving mode."

In my heart, I was thinking, *Now here's a guy who doesn't know about my spiritual heritage. I've seen the lame walk and demons cast out, and he's telling me how to hold my hands.* I was offended and felt prideful but endured the rest of his prayer.

When he finished, I was still feeling as empty as when I had come in. I walked away from the line and stood by one of the building's many support posts and began venting to God. I was frustrated and angry. I knew God was doing something, but I just couldn't receive it.

At the hotel room, I asked my dad questions about the meeting that night. I was trying to find a thread of hope for myself but still felt I was missing the point.

I said, "Dad, what do you think this is? Did God touch you tonight?"

My father's response was different from what I expected.

"Son, I know it's different than what we're used to, but I saw a lady praying and I sensed the Lord on her. I don't know about the rest of this, and I don't care for some of this, but I saw something on her tonight."

I agreed to return a second night with my father. To my dismay, the service was the same. The Arnotts were still gone and the worship team had not returned. No one bothered to retype the scribbled words on the overhead projector. The sermon was good yet simple. And once again I missed my window to make it to the front of the building. I went to the back to receive prayer. Afterwards I felt the same as the night before. I found myself leaning against my favorite pole, complaining to God.

My father walked toward me.

"I'm ready to go," I declared.

"Come with me, son," he said patiently. "I found the lady I told you about last night. I want you to watch her pray for people. Maybe we could catch for her."

I hesitantly decided to go with my father. For a while and from a distance I watched what happened when she prayed. People started trembling and fell over. Some wept; others laughed. We moved closer to her and ended up catching people as they fell to the ground.

Her prayers were so simple but sweet. She would say, "I ask, Jesus, that You would wash Your Spirit over this person. Give them more of You. Wash them with Your presence and fill them with Your fire." The person would start to shake and then fall to the floor.

As we began to move from person to person, I sensed the power of God. I had positioned myself with my hand against the middle of each person's back to catch them. As they trembled, I could feel the power of God sweep over me. It was something I had experienced as a boy. While everything else seemed so different in the service, I recognized the familiar presence of God. I started crying, and when I looked at my father I saw tears rushing down his cheeks. We continued to catch for the rest of the evening. At the end we asked her to pray for us. While I didn't feel what others had felt, I couldn't stop crying.

On the third night, we caught for the same lady and asked her to pray for us again. I must add that this was unusual for me, because I thought it was juvenile to pursue these sorts of things. At this point in my life I believed that anyone who was full of the Spirit of God could receive all of God they needed in their private time of prayer with the Lord. But God was humbling me and showing me that this was Church Body ministry.

I fell to the floor under God's presence. The woman stayed with me and put her hand on my head. She prayed for what seemed like hours and began speaking the Word of the Lord over me and reaffirmed things He had already spoken to me. She also addressed my pride. Something deep began happening in me that night and before I left the church, I picked up two worship CDs.

The tears followed me back to Nashville where the movers were waiting to transfer my furniture to Pensacola. It was April 1995. Two songs—"Draw Me Close" and "You Are Worthy"—were set to repeat in my CD player. Each time I listened to them I began to weep.

God began a deep work of repentance in me that lasted more than two tear-stained weeks. He pulled layer after layer of pride and spiritual arrogance from me. He pulled off religion, so I could embrace relationship with Him. The whole time the movers packed, these two songs played in the background and I wept uncontrollably. The movers must have thought I was chronically depressed!

When we allow God to begin digging around in the layers of our hearts, we will find many things we never imagined were there. Upon discovering them, we are filled with anguish, repentance and wonder at how we could have collected them. This was especially true of me because I had been in the church my whole life.

Once I arrived in Pensacola I discovered that all the people who had gone to Toronto shared a deep, common bond. We had struggled with the same issues—spiritual pride and hunger for God—but each of us had walked away with an experience that would change us for years to come. We knew that God had kissed our souls and refreshed us in ways we didn't completely understand.

Revival was still two months away at Brownsville, but there was a stirring in our hearts. There was a new hunger among the leadership and those who made the trip to Toronto. The congregation of Brownsville had been praying for revival for over two and a half years, so the whole church had a certain level of expectation.

Our hunger continued to grow. We would find ourselves at Pastor Kilpatrick's house, sitting on the screened porch. One by one we would share the story of what God had done for us in Toronto. Like those on the road to Emmaus, we found our hearts stirring within us. We would well up with tears and His Spirit would visit us. We prayed for one another, fell under God's power and experienced His glorious presence. One of the young women who joined us, Amber Linkenhoker, would later become my wife.

Ironically, the refreshing that was happening on the pastor's back porch wasn't yet happening in the church. John recognized this but spoke very directly. He told us we couldn't manufacture what was happening; we had to wait until God sovereignly did it. That's why I personally believe revival came to Brownsville a month before Father's Day. Rather than two-hour prayer meetings, people were beginning to linger. There were nights when John would sit on the stage and kids from the church would just crawl up on his lap and listen to the worship. We were a big family.

I began to sing new worship choruses from the albums I heard in Toronto and people would linger to just stay in the presence of the Lord. We were waiting for Him to come. This was something new, because church as I had come to know it was more along the lines of performing your duty as a minister and going out to eat afterwards or getting home in time to catch your favorite program.

This waiting was wonderful and full of expectancy. We were driven by a definable hunger and a grasping of Scriptures like 2 Chronicles 7:14 (*NKJV*): "If my people who are called by My name will humble themselves, and pray and seek My face and turn from their wicked ways, then I will hear from heaven, and will forgive their sin and heal their land." The sweetness of the

Lord would cause some of us to weep, but it caused all of us to worship more deeply than we had ever done before.

The Western Church has a desire to always label everything and to draw lines and come to conclusions about whether or not what is happening is of God or Satan. Toronto has been called a refreshing, a blessing and an outpouring. I am cautious to label it anything other than a move of the Holy Spirit. It may even be revival, because isn't revival designed to revive and bring the Church back to its first love? That seems to be the fruit that remains.

If someone hears of something from a second or third source, he can be convinced that it may or may not be a good thing; but he who has seen and tasted it himself cannot be convinced otherwise. Since March 1995, my hunger for the Lord has increased and my passion to know Jesus is greater than ever before. I now live as a man driven to see the face of my Lord, and I can understand more clearly what Paul meant when he said in Philippians 3:8, "I count all things to be loss in view of the surpassing value of knowing Christ Jesus my Lord."

# life-defining moment

## JACK TAYLOR

*Jack Taylor came to Toronto in the summer of 1994, while we were still at our little place near the corner of Derry and Dixie Roads. I remember Randy Clark telling me that Jack, a prominent Southern Baptist and former vice president of that great denomination, had been to our meetings and was mightily touched by God. He had been in revival before, and when he came to Toronto, he recognized instantly that this was God. Jack and his wife, Barbara, in ministry together for more than half a century, spent 25 of those years in pastorates in Texas. Today, Jack is the author of 13 books. He and his wife are based in Melbourne, Florida, and have an international speaking ministry. —J. A.*

In August 1994, seven months after the events that marked the beginning of the Toronto Blessing, I was drawn to go see this spiritual phenomenon. My wife and I, together with an elder from our church, arrived in Toronto and registered in a little nondescript motel across from the industrial plaza where the church held its meetings. Barbara and I looked out our window and saw people in the parking lot and realized they were gathering for church. By the time we hurriedly got ready and joined the crowd, there was a line halfway around the building. For the first time in my life, I stood in line to go to church! Those who waited with us were visiting from around the world. We passed the time together sharing about the work of God in the Church and in our own lives.

An hour later the doors opened, and the church filled rapidly. The moment we walked in, I sensed what I had felt during a great move of God 25 years earlier in my own church in San Antonio, Texas. In 1969, the Holy Spirit had graciously visited our congregation, and as many as 2,000 people were saved in the following six months. On this day, once again, the presence of God was so real that I could not hold back the tears during both the worship and the preaching.

# preparing for refreshment

At the end of the service we were asked to lend a hand in stacking the chairs against the walls—all the floor space would be needed! Then the visiting pastors and leaders were invited to step forward to receive prayer. For the first time I was seeing a form of ministry that I felt was both scriptural and anointed. Not just one person, but a whole team waited at the front for those who were coming forward. I confess that I wanted the preacher to pray for me, but I couldn't get to him. I would head toward him and he would go the other way! Instead, a precious lady quietly and humbly prayed for me.

The next thing I knew, I was on the floor along with many others. My wife was beside me, tears flowing down her face and onto the carpet. I thought, *My friends already think I've blown a spiritual gasket; what are they going to think now?* My questions soon vanished in a deep and thorough peace. God had my full attention. It had been a long time since God had me all to Himself. What a good position from which to listen to what He had to say!

The Lord began to speak to me, and His first words were "I am lowering your cholesterol and cleaning out your arteries." Physical healing was one of the last things on my mind as a purpose for this journey, although five years earlier my open-heart surgery had been followed by complications, infections and a near-death experience. When I recovered from the surgery, I had considered myself to be in good health. As I lay there, I welcomed all that God wanted to do, but this seemed somewhat shallow in the light of my other expectations.

The next thing I heard was "What I am doing in you physically will illustrate what I am doing in you spiritually." Without knowing what this involved, I simply consented. I knew that heart problems were related to cholesterol and blocked arteries, but there was no major revelation of the significance of what He had spoken.

## Fresh Filling

At the meeting the next night, my wife broke into laughter that lasted almost two hours! She testified to an inner healing and a peace beyond anything she had ever known.

These days were a fresh filling of the Spirit for us. We discovered at the Toronto church a safe place where the Holy Spirit could do a new work in us. The atmosphere was charged with the power and presence of God, and the servant spirits of the ones ministering drew us to a new level in Him. We had felt the same sweet rush of His love, peace and power in the move of God in the early '70s; once again we felt we were being swept along on the crest of a tidal wave.

In the afternoons I was blessed by the ministry of Guy Chevreau. His teaching sessions were enormously helpful for those of us who were learning to navigate new waters. He connected this movement to legitimate historical movements and so validated the authenticity of what God was doing in Toronto. It became very clear that in recording the histories of revivals, we have tended to omit many documented manifestations that might make us uncomfortable.

## Fresh Deliverance

At that time I would have told you I had freedom in the things of the Lord. The truth is, there were unresolved roots of Pharisaism in me. I was critical of anything I could not understand by reason. I was willing to part company with anyone with whom I differed on doctrinal details. I had negative feelings regarding those who gave in to extreme manifestations. But in those moments on the floor in Toronto, I was being delivered of the roots of religion. A religious spirit was losing place in me.

I had the opportunity to have my cholesterol level checked in a local clinic. The result? My cholesterol was 45 points lower than on my previous test! My faith was strengthened; since God had done this in me physically, surely He had also done in me spiritually what He had promised.

Looking back on that episode, I now realize that for the first time in 47 years of ministry and 51 years of being a Christian, I had given God the right to do anything He wanted, in any way He wanted to do it, *without offending me*. My previous offense level was extremely high. But since that visit I have had a total peace with what is happening around me, even when I do not understand it all. I now have the certainty that whether it is of God, the flesh or the devil, my Father can handle it.

## Fresh Revelation

I live a few yards from the beach and can hear the pounding surf of the mighty Atlantic Ocean. On this morning I walked outside to photograph one of our sensational sunrises. I noticed again what I first learned when we became shore dwellers: The roar of the surf is caused by the clash of old waves going out and new waves coming in. This understanding has served to caution me against fighting new waves of the Spirit that may be unlike those I have seen in the earlier days of my ministry. No two works of God are the same. He is original, innovative and wonderfully diverse. He is sovereign; He can do anything He wants to do, in any way He wants to do it and always be right. My first visit to the Toronto Blessing reinforced for me this facet of the sovereignty of God.

## A Refreshed Ministry

Our time in Toronto marked an increase in joy and anointing in ministry. A few months after our trip we went back again for a second visit. Shortly after that I received a call from John Arnott, whom I had not yet had the opportunity to meet. John invited me to accompany him on a trip to England. There I saw first-hand the influence of the Toronto Blessing. Thousands of believers had gone to Toronto to get in the river, and now they were letting the river flow in their own nation. For three consecutive years I visited England and was surprised and delighted to see the responses of the "staid" British to the work of God among them.

At a time when my culture says I should be slowing down and planning to retire, my expectation and excitement are greater than ever. Since 1995, it has been my pleasure to preach on different occasions at the Toronto Airport Christian Fellowship and to work with John and Carol Arnott in conferences across America. After my journeys to Toronto, God made it very clear to me there would come a time in America when no one would have to travel outside his or her county or parish to see a genuine work of God. That promise is coming true across the United States in Florida, Missouri, Vermont, Massachusetts, Washington State, New Jersey, Oregon, Texas and California. Many of these current moves of God's Spirit have early connections to the Toronto Blessing.

# pastoring a move of God

In my study of revival movements throughout history, I have noted that most have lasted no longer than three years and that many have been diverted to extremism, heretical teachings and even immorality. Even in the most spiritual of endeavors, there may be indications of the flesh. This present move, however, seems to be more balanced as it grows. The maturity of the whole Toronto team over the past seven years has not only kept their local move of the Spirit on track but has also served as a model for pastoring a move of God. The Lord is sovereign, but He guides pastors and leaders to preside over these works and to give understanding and direction to folks who might otherwise give in to dangerous human excesses.

John and Carol Arnott, amid the rushing of this river of blessings and under a continuing barrage of criticism, have maintained a level of integrity and balance that has helped protect and sustain a mighty work of God.

I put much stock in the testimonies of real people. Accompanying us on our second trip to Toronto was Gary Folds, a Baptist pastor who had never seen manifestations such as he saw during that visit. Were it not for our friendship, he normally would have been violently opposed to these phenomena. At first he declined my invitation to join our group of 30, saying that he was just "not ready for that stuff." At the last minute he changed his mind and came with us. Watching him during those days was a study in human responses! Initially he was turned off; then he became trustful of God's ability to keep things in order. Next, he was open but cautious and, finally, he was desirous that something would happen to him! Nothing significant transpired on that trip, but he returned home with a decided openness to the things of the Spirit. He went back to his church and spoke favorably of what he had seen in Toronto.

A few months later I invited Gary to attend revival meetings with Randy Clark in our area here in Melbourne. God touched Gary, and his life was permanently altered. Every now and then when we fellowship together I say to him, "Gary, if there were no other proof of the validity of what is happening in Toronto than your life and ministry, that would be enough for me."

To those who have judged the move that began in Toronto in 1994, claiming that it is not of God, I simply say, "I can only report to you what I have witnessed, heard and personally experienced, which has enhanced my life, my family's life and my ministry." To John and Carol and the Toronto Airport Christian Fellowship, thank you for your faithfulness, authenticity and perseverance. Most of all, thank You, Father, for answering our prayers to revive us again!

# changed by the Father's love

TERRY MOORE

*Former businessman Terry Moore is the senior pastor of Sojourn Church in Carrollton, Texas. We met him when he came to Toronto, near the beginning of the revival, with several pastor friends from the Dallas-Fort Worth area. We have since been to his church several times, as well as to citywide conferences held in Dallas. Terry and his wife, Susan, are precious pastors who have been wonderfully blessed by a fresh touch of the Holy Spirit. —J. A.*

Since God changed my life in an encounter with the Holy Spirit in August 1982, my heart's desire has been to know Him more. In 1994 we heard that a powerful move of God was taking place in Toronto and our curiosity turned into genuine interest. We had no desire to chase the latest spiritual fad, but we did want to be a part of any authentic activity of the Holy Spirit.

I spoke with the elders of our church; several were eager to visit the revival as soon as possible, even though we did not know much about it. Because we were leaving on short notice, we ended up traveling in two groups. Several left almost immediately for Toronto, and the rest of us met them there.

When the first group got to Canada, they sent back reports that the Holy Spirit was indeed moving mightily. They were being touched and changed in His presence and were awestruck by what God was doing. Their excitement was contagious. A few days later, I boarded a plane with my wife, Susan, and some others from our church and headed north. We made the trip with a tremendous sense of anticipation, eager to experience the outpouring of the Spirit.

Having grown up in a Southern Baptist family, I was familiar with the terms "revival" and "a mighty move of God." In my mind, a revival took place when large numbers responded to what the Lord was doing—typified by crowded altars full of people receiving Jesus, rededication of lives to Him or committing themselves to the ministry. *I* understood revival and expected the services in Toronto to fit my definition. My ideas were about to be challenged.

We arrived to a beautiful snowfall and settled into our hotel rooms quickly. The service was scheduled to begin at 7:30, so we arrived before 6:00, prepared to stand in line, bundled in our winter coats. But the only person we saw was a woman praying in the nursery area.

As we entered the sanctuary, we still did not see many people. At 7:20, most of the seats were still empty. I was a little perplexed. We had traveled a long distance and had sacrificed both time and money to experience God in a fresh and powerful way. I wondered, *If God is so active and so mighty in this place, why aren't more people here?* We sat down and introduced ourselves to a couple sitting nearby. They were from Arlington, Texas. So we had flown several hours and hundreds of miles to meet one intercessor in an empty nursery and two people from the town next to us back home! This was not at all what I had envisioned.

By the time the service began at 7:30, there were about 200 people in the sanctuary, which would hold 300 or more. Pastor John Arnott and his wife, Carol, entered the room with no hype or fanfare and began greeting people individually, making us all feel perfectly welcome and comfortable. The praise started, but within a few moments something happened that I had not expected. As we worshiped, the Holy Spirit began to fill the room. When I first sensed His presence, I said to the Lord in my heart, *This is You!* He responded, "Do you think I've changed?" Of course He hadn't changed. I recognized when the Holy Spirit entered a room, and His presence here was unmistakable. It was the sweet, rich, holy presence that only He possesses. If this was revival, then revival was not necessarily what I had always believed it to be! It was going to be an interesting evening.

After the music, John welcomed everyone and asked where we lived. I was astounded to find out that in such a small group, people had come from several different nations. Sensing the presence of the Holy Spirit and listening to those who had come from distant places, I thought, *Maybe, just maybe, something can happen here after all.* Maybe God could move just as mightily among 200 people as He could among 200,000!

John spoke for several minutes, asked for testimonies and then moved into a time of ministry. Before he began to pray for people, he gave two instructions I had not heard before. First, he told us if we fell down under the power of the Holy Spirit, we should not try to get back up immediately. Instead, he instructed us to ask the Holy Spirit if there was anything else He wanted to do. We were to stay in His presence and not rush anything He might be working in our lives. We were to be patient and linger with Him. John called this soaking—simply allowing the Holy Spirit to saturate us with His presence. Second, John encouraged us to be prayed for more than once. He wanted us to keep receiving prayer so that we would stay open to everything God had for us during the ministry time.

I was prayed for during each of the six services we attended. That first night, I ended up, like most others, flat on my back. The carpet had seen better days, and in the Canadian winter the floor was cold! The presence of the Lord was so sweet, and my spirit perceived a work of the Holy Spirit in my heart, but my mind did not totally comprehend it. Not until I returned to Dallas did I realize what God had begun to do in my life and what the lasting fruit of the Toronto experience would be.

As we flew home that Saturday, the first group to visit Toronto had already returned and word of their experiences had spread quickly. One elder had been especially blessed by the joy of the Lord. After God touched him, he had laughed for 12 hours straight! When things like that happen in a church body, people find out in a hurry. I planned to report on our trip during the morning service the following day and let everyone know what God was doing in Toronto. Their curiosity and anticipation were high.

We used natural words to try to describe supernatural experiences, but we could not adequately communicate everything that had happened in our spirits. Instead of giving a report on our trip, those of us who had been to Toronto wanted to simply invite the Holy Spirit to come among us and then pray for the people in our church. We shared the two things we had learned: allow the Holy Spirit to minister everything He has, and keep getting prayed for. We started praying about noon, and God began to move. As He did, our congregation responded in a variety of ways. Some were weeping, others were laughing, and others were simply in awe of His presence. Still others, however, were offended by this outpouring.

We prayed for people until about 3:00 that afternoon. Many received an unusual touch from the Lord as the Holy Spirit ministered healing, wholeness and joy. Our church had been deeply changed by the sweet and mighty presence of our God. He had begun to release a revelation of the love of the Father, showing us what it really means to belong to Him. He was giving us a fresh understanding of His heart for us as His children, whom He loves passionately, patiently and without limit. He was imparting to us the "Spirit of adoption by whom we cry out 'Abba, Father'" (Rom. 8:15, *NKJV*). He was revealing to us the tenderness, the grace, the mercy and the power of His love in a manner that would forever change the way we thought about Him and the way we thought about ourselves.

That Sunday night as I spoke with others in our church who had been to Toronto, the question arose, What should we do now? The church had been so impacted that day that we decided to gather the next night for a time of worship and prayer, and see if God would show up again. And show up He did! We decided to start holding nightly services that would include worship, prayer and ministry. If the Lord gave us the grace to continue night after night, we would. If we did not sense His anointing, we would discontinue the meetings.

That first Monday night meeting went well. I could not attend the service because of a previously scheduled commitment out of town. I returned in time for the Tuesday night meeting and was excited about it but felt inadequate to lead the service. It seemed to me that Susan and one of the elders who had traveled with us to Toronto had received more than I did. So after the praise and worship, I was the first one to be prayed for.

Again, I ended up on the floor, this time with a tangible sensation of someone's hand gently but heavily placed on my chest. I knew it was the Lord, although I had never before felt Him in such a physical way. I felt that Jesus, our intercessor, was praying for me Himself. I sensed that He was ministering to me so deeply and so personally that I was being permanently changed right there on the floor. His nearness was indescribable. Although I was confident that the Lord was touching me, I opened one eye to see whose hand was on my chest. No one was there! *It was my Father.* It was the hand of the Lord touching me in a way that I could feel, releasing a greater measure of His fatherly affection, pleasure and devotion than I had ever known.

From that moment on, I have walked in an unshakable confidence in His love. He has made me sensitive to the working of the Holy Spirit in all sorts of situations, from personal prayer times at home to times when I am sitting in a meeting. Since that night, I have been thoroughly convinced, as was the apostle Paul, "that neither death nor life, nor angels nor principalities nor powers, nor things present nor things to come, nor height nor depth, nor any other created thing, shall be able to separate us from the love of God which is in Christ Jesus our Lord" (Rom. 8:38,39, *NKJV*).

Our church does not hold nightly meetings anymore, but while we did, the Lord established us in His love as a congregation. I believe that one of the hallmarks of Sojourn Church is our experience with the love of the Father. We have become known as a place of healing and hope, a place where people can encounter the Lord as their Father and experience His love in a profound and life-changing way.

My prayer today is that God would continue to give His people an increasing revelation of His lavish love. I pray that He would continue to pour out more and more of His presence. Before I went to Toronto, I cannot say that my heart was desperately crying out for the revelation I received. But God knew my heart. He knew I was hungry for more of Him. We must trust Him to see into the places in our hearts that we may be unaware of and to answer the prayers we have not even spoken. He sees our struggles, and as a compassionate Father, He wants to help and heal us.

I have come to understand that revival does not require a mass gathering of people; it simply requires a touch from the Father. In a relatively small gathering at a church in Toronto, the Holy Spirit began a work in my heart that revealed the Father's love and changed me forever. Because there are no limits to His love, that revelation continues to transform me and, I pray, will continue to change me forever.

# "i saw Jesus"

## DICK AND BETTY MILLS

*Dick and Betty Mills have been a part of the charismatic renewal since 1966. Dick is well known to the Body of Christ for his amazing gift of prophesying encouraging words to people while quoting only Scripture. Carol and I met Dick in 1982, soon after we had started our first church, in Stratford, Ontario. He gave us a word at that time that we would have "much people in the city" and that our ministry would produce a harvest of 30-, then 60- and finally 100-fold. We heard little of him after that, but in November 1999, I felt strangely prompted to call him. My secretary, Petra, easily found him and I was surprised to learn that he too had been to Toronto and had been wonderfully blessed. Dick was thrilled to be reminded of his prophetic word to us 18 years earlier and to realize that God was more than fulfilling that word! To this day, Carol carries Dick's word in her Bible. —J. A.*

Many, many years ago, the Lord met me in a profound way that clearly showed His purposes for me as a servant in His kingdom. At that time I was slain in the Spirit, and for two hours I saw a great unfolding of the end times and what I could expect to happen. I also had a visible encounter with the Lord Jesus Christ. He forgave me of my backsliding and restored the joy of my salvation. I was refilled with the blessed Holy Spirit. Peace of mind was given to me and an anointing was imparted for me to travel with the good news of the gospel.

While reveling in God's abounding compassion and graciousness, the Lord began to reveal to me seven moves of the Holy

Spirit that I would experience in my lifetime. He said that I would recognize them sometimes as a sideline observer and sometimes as a participant. But the main purpose of this unfolding drama was for me to persevere and patiently wait for the last move He had revealed to me. The Lord was personalizing my call to let me know what was coming in the future and how I could fit into His scheme of things. That was the year 1943.

Since that time, I have been a witness to all the moves He revealed to me. I am speaking of latter rain, the healing evangelists, the charismatic renewal, the para-church groups, the word of faith movement, and the third wave (plus the river groups— Pensacola, Tampa, Smithton, Van Nuys and Toronto). I'm only trying to give you a rundown on what I've seen and experienced myself between my calling in 1943 and what is happening as we start the new millennium. I am not going to critique any of the moves for weaknesses or strengths. I'm only listing them to share what I've see, heard and felt.

# a new move of the Spirit

And now we come to the Father's Blessing. I would like to relate to you a divine encounter I had at the Toronto Airport Christian Fellowship (TACF) while pastor John Arnott was speaking. Pastor John was sharing some renewal testimonies. I was sitting in the audience listening and enjoying him tell of all the good things the Lord was doing. The Holy Spirit was present. The audience of several thousand were very attentive. The worship produced the high praises recorded in Psalm 149:6. Pastor Arnott was speaking with a very clear anointing.

It was my first time at TACF and I was rapt with the very awareness of the Lord being there in power and glory. Without any preparation on my part or any forewarning by the Lord, I saw Pastor John's face disappear. The face of Jesus was superimposed on the very spot that Pastor John's face was before this happened. Jesus looked right at me and said, "It is time for the seventh move to begin." That's all He said. His face disappeared and again I was conscious of Pastor John speaking and continuing on with his message.

What do I anticipate and what Scriptures do I stand on for even believing there will be another outpouring of the Holy Spirit and that part of this outpouring is through TACF? Romans 9:28 says that it will be a short, terse, succinct, final summary act of righteousness. It will climax the Church age with the second coming of Christ. Isaiah 29:14 states that the Lord will do a powerful and miraculous work that will leave the wise and prudent of this world's system speechless and without an explanation of what is happening.

This is happening in Toronto. I am impressed with the fact that TACF considers itself a John the Baptist type of ministry. I've heard Pastor John say repeatedly "We're not the final move of God; we're called like John the Baptist to prepare the way for the Lord's appearance to His Church."

There is no doubt that I saw Jesus at TACF. By the time you read this I will have been to Toronto three times. The quest for more of Him is still very intense. The need for more intimacy with the Lord at the personal level is still held up as the believer's ideal. And the expectancy for the new wave has never waned. In fact, it is more intense now than it was five years ago.

My wife, Betty, also had a life-changing experience at TACF. We would like to tell you of one night when the Lord touched her deeply and restored memories that had been lost to her since early childhood. Betty's story will show you how the Lord tailors his touch in a very personal and loving way to make His children whole.

# how betty mills met Jesus at TACF

As I write this part of the testimony, Betty is filling me in on the details and I'm writing her recollection of that wonderful night at Toronto Airport Christian Fellowship (TACF). I am also putting down my observations of the tremendous encounter Betty had with the Lord Jesus Christ. I just hope we can convey to you an event that revolutionized both of our lives.

This has to do with what the TACF staff call soaking prayers. After the regular services, attendees who come to Toronto for ministry lineup, standing on the red line marked for ministry. A couple people (sometimes more than two) will single out a person who wants prayer and quietly begin the soaking prayer. Sometimes it lasts 5 minutes, sometimes 15 minutes, and sometimes it can go 30 minutes if necessary. The person being prayed for will slump to the ground and be stretched out on the floor. No one is pushing the person over; it's a manifestation of the Holy Spirit.

A person being overwhelmed by the Holy Spirit's presence can be described as rapt with ecstasy, resting in the Spirit, doing carpet time, the slain of the Lord, being in a swoon, being in a coma, a paroxysm of conviction, under the power, slain in the Spirit, being out, and/or being on God's operating table. Someone even wrote a chorus about all this. "I'm under the spout where the glory comes out."

It's only a theory, but I feel that what is happening is a release of God's glory that is more than the human frame can cope with. The word for "glory" in the Old Testament is *kabod*. It means a heavy, dense, glorious splendor. When the heavy, radiant glory of God impacts a person, the frail human being can't remain standing. This happened to Saul of Tarsus on his way to Damascus. In Acts 9:3,4, the glory was so bright that Saul fell to the ground.

At TACF, the time spent on the floor is called carpet time. It is considered a very sacred moment because the person lying there is under the jurisdiction of the Holy Spirit. Spiritual things start happening at that moment. Some people have dreams; some have visions; healings occur; answers to unresolved problems happen. Some people receive a call to the ministry. Some receive an impartation of spiritual gifts. It is not possible to name all the things that might happen; but believe me, wonderful things are going on in the heart and life of the one lying there in the presence of the Lord.

Betty was one of those ministered to with the soaking prayer. She fell to the floor and a tremendous sequence of events started happening that she later told me about. We've been married 43 years and, coming from a Baptist background, she was not familiar with this phenomenon. I should say that we both had an unusual experience at Melodyland Christian Center one time. In the late '70s, the late Kathryn Kuhlman was speaking on a Monday night. We were sitting in the front row in the middle seats between two aisles. Kathryn left the platform to walk out because the service was closing. When she got to the aisle, she stopped and looked at us both. While we were sitting there watching her, her gaze struck our eyes. At that moment our feet went out and our bodies catapulted to the altar, feet first like a cannon shot. We weren't hurt. It was very ecstatic and we both felt the glory of the Lord. It lasted less than a minute because someone helped us up to our feet, and we left with all the other departing folks who had come to the meeting.

In the Toronto meeting things were so different. Betty laid on the floor for over 20 minutes. Standing there watching all this was a great experience for me. She had an angelic smile, and with her eyes closed she seemed to be watching an unfolding drama. Betty has a regal bearing and demeanor. I tell her often that she reminds me of the queen of England. We laugh and say, "Not as rich as the queen of England financially" (reportedly worth $7 billion); but in so many other ways Betty *is* regal, carrying herself with a natural dignity combined with a spiritual beauty.

That night at TACF, something happened that changed Betty's whole life. She lay there looking very dignified and to me looking very beautiful. Words fail me when trying to express the radiant heavenly look on her face. I'm relying on Betty's recollections to tell what happened during that 20-minute period on the floor.

To give you some background, Betty couldn't relate to the Lord's Prayer. She drew a blank on "Our Father which art in heaven." She couldn't relate to the "Our Father" part.

Betty had grown up on a southern Illinois farm, the 8th of 10 children. The death of her father when she was seven years old was so painful that she was unable to remember anything that happened in the father/daughter relationship for the first seven years of her life.

J. B. Phillips, in his book *Your God Is Too Small*, says in so many words that our concept of God as Father will be determined by our relationship with our earthly father. If your earthly father was too busy for you, God will be too busy for you. If your earthly father was too cruel, your heavenly Father will seem too cruel. If your earthly father was loving and affectionate, it will be easy for you to see your heavenly Father as loving and affectionate. Since Betty had literally grown up without a father and because the first seven years were blocked out by memory lapse, it's easy to understand why one of God's redeemed saints was not able to link with "Our Father which art in heaven."

All this changed during our visit to TACF. In those 20 minutes on the floor, the Lord gave Betty a review of the seven missing years. Do you remember the TV series *This Is Your Life*? The Lord did that for her; it was like rewinding a VCR tape back to the beginning and playing it over. She told me that she was shown many things her father did with her. (Recently, while in St. Louis, Missouri, two of her sisters told me that Betty was her father's favorite.) She saw that he read bedtime stories to her. He let her ride with him on the big tractor. He would bounce her up and down. He offered to cut a wart off of her finger if she would give him a bite of her cookie. She saw him laughing joyously with her, walking down the country lane with her and praying with her. All that had been obliterated from her memory bank by his traumatic death had been given back.

———

I love the words "Toronto Blessing." Betty and I are only two of the tens of thousands who have traveled to TACF and been blessed. We know that God led us there. For me it was a wake-up call to get ready for another great outpouring of the Holy Spirit. For Betty it was an inner healing—going down memory lane and having the Lord fill in the blank spaces in the photograph album of her mind. What a wonderful Savior we have!

Every time I go back to TACF, I go with the confidence that Jesus is there to meet the spiritual hunger and thirst that I find in His people everywhere I go. If you want more out of life than your Christian experience is currently providing, I suggest you make the trip to Toronto Airport Fellowship and do like the psalmist David suggested: "Oh taste and see that the Lord is good" (Ps. 34:8).

# the Father's blessing and inner healing

## JOHN AND PAULA SANDFORD

*John and Paula Sandford are loved throughout the world for their ministry of emotional healing and their best-selling books* Transformation of the Inner Man *and* Healing the Wounded Spirit. *Their ministry has had a profound impact on Carol and me. For years, we have incorporated their teachings as a necessary element of our leaders' training track. They came to do a conference with us in the fall of 1994, something that had been booked two years prior. Meanwhile, revival had broken out in our church. They came and taught for us and were mightily impacted themselves. We were so impressed by the eagerness and humility of this seasoned ministry couple—they taught all day and then would come to the evening meetings and stand on our prayer lines! God wonderfully touched them as our prayer team ministered to them. —J. A.*

Paula and I were among the first in the old-line churches to receive the baptism of the Holy Spirit. For that we took a lot of ridicule and persecution from liberals. But that was nothing compared to the rejections, slanders and persecutions from religious born-anew Christians when we began to teach and write about inner healing. In the beginning it was like plowing cement with our noses! Many simply could not understand that after we receive Jesus and are born anew, the work of being transformed into Christ's nature has not ended; it has only begun. Most have thought that denial is a river in Egypt!

In 1974, we founded Elijah House—a nonprofit, international organization committed to restoration and healing of lives and relationships as expressed in the principles found in Malachi 4:5,6 and Matthew 17:11. Elijah House also focuses on equipping the Body of Christ to encourage others and share the healing love of Father God. Now there are Elijah Houses in Australia, New Zealand, Finland, Austria and Canada, and a large number of affiliates.

The years of labor and the many persecutions and slander took their toll, however. We were worn out and hungry for more of the Lord, just to survive. In October 1994, we came to Toronto to teach a seminar for John and Carol Arnott. We taught 700 people during the day and basked with 1,000 in the presence of the Lord each night. The wondrous refreshing presence of the Father through the Holy Spirit began to sweep away the years of accumulated fatigue and sorrow. For the first time, we began to feel the fullness of the joy of the Lord, which we had only tasted sparingly now and then.

Paula testified that when lying on the floor, it felt as though she were floating in a gentle river of the Lord's love—and, of course, she was, as prophesied in Ezekiel 47! I received a major healing as the burden for my father and mother's relationship was finally lifted out of my heart. I knew with my head that I didn't have to save them, but my heart hadn't been able to let go. Now I had the assurance and peace that the Lord had it all in His hands. We learned at heart level what our minds knew and our mouths had so often preached—that Jesus really is the living Lord, the One who is taking the initiative to act among men for their salvation. We had been trying too hard to help God out. But the power of His presence taught us that He is truly on the job, that He *will* sanctify His Church in His own way and time.

The upshot of the Father's Blessing in Toronto was that we were brought into a deeper dimension of rest. "There remains therefore a Sabbath rest for the people of God. For the one who has entered *His rest has himself also rested from his works*, as God did from His" (Heb. 4:9,10, emphasis added). Despite how many times we had told ourselves and others that God is God, that He is at work for His good pleasure and ours, our tardy hearts really thought it was mostly up to us. We were fond of saying "I know it's God who raises the garden, but you should have seen it when He had it alone!" It took the power of the Lord's love cascading over and through us to teach our hearts that He really is the One in charge, doing the work, whether in and through us or through others. At last we could let go and know beyond knowing that God is surely acting in all of human history and that He can do quite well enough without our help. We have the joy of being unnecessary, yet we have the privilege of participating anyway!

The Father's Blessing restored us to the reality of the love of Jesus. The biblical and theological truth of His love for us had never left us; it's what kept us going all those years. But we needed to *experience* His love more fully, more often. We are now much more in love with Jesus than ever before. His Presence saturates us with God's love every day. He refreshes and revitalizes our walk in Him as often as we turn to Him. Still, every once in a while we find we need to run back up to Toronto to bathe anew in the river we find there, where friends come around and once more pour in His love, and worship lifts our spirits from the humdrum to the glorious all over again.

We see now that people need more and more of the Father's love so that fear can be cast away and the wheels of insight and ministry greased by the Holy Spirit. Only then can they receive the depths of inner healing that produce transformation into Jesus' nature. The more healing and transformation occur, the more of the Father's love people can receive. Sometimes that is all we need. The Father's love drives out fear; then we see our broken places, we confess, we die anew on the Cross and are set free. But it is not that simple because we are not always aware of what is hidden in our hearts (see 1 Cor. 4:4,5). The more we experience the Lord's presence and unconditional love, the more He makes us capable of recognizing and dealing with the hidden and hurtful things still lodged deep within.

> Search me, O God, and know my heart; try me and know
> my anxious thoughts; and see if there be any hurtful way
> in me, and lead me in the everlasting way (Ps. 139:23,24).

As we respond to the Holy Spirit's timely revelations of sin *in* us as well as *against* us and consciously take those things to the Cross through repentance and forgiveness, we know more and more fully the reality of His work of sanctification and transformation. Our ability to receive and fully experience the wonderful gift of God's love then multiplies because we can receive so much more. Then, as inner healing brings revelation upon revelation, our hearts are open to more love and more revelations in repeated cycles of blessing. The Father's Blessing and inner healing operate together to mature and equip the Body of Christ to serve the Lord according to *His* agenda.

# God's purposes

God's purposes are of greater magnitude and importance than comforting and healing individual lives, important as that is. We believe that the relationship between renewal and inner healing ministry is a major key to the fulfillment of many of the other moves of God in our time.

## Intercession

Intercession begins in the heart of God. Intercession is not us begging or manipulating God to do something He is reluctant to do or doesn't want to do. True intercession is a response to His call, inviting Him to do what He has already purposed. For that, we must be able to hear Him clearly, so we can pray according to His will. If we are to grow in our ability to hear His voice, we must develop the kind of intimate relationship with Him that enables change. Without sufficient cleansing and healing of our hearts, we may see and hear inaccurately. With unhealed eyes and ears, we may project our own problems and agendas, or our need to fix things, onto people and situations that are not yet ripe. The trouble we see may be real, but what we want to pray about it may not be God's will. We need to hear in each instance what God wants to do, when He wants to do it and where and how He wants to do it.

His love not only enables hearing, but it also creates the ability to be corporate with others and to hear their counsel. Humility to check with others concerning their hearing and hunches is not only wise, but it's also often imperative. If we have not experienced enough of His loving and powerful presence, we may hesitate to trust others corporately. We count ourselves blessed to have learned in Toronto to soak in the presence of the Lord, and we have carried that gift home. We are also blessed that our children share dreams and visions, prophetic words and scriptural guidance with us—as do people on our staff, individuals in our home fellowship group and friends around the world. It is the combination of the Father's love and the deeper application of inner healing that enables us to profit from all that our children and friends share with us.

## Deliverance

Through repentance and forgiveness, the practiced character structures within us—which can serve as houses for the demonic—are put to death on the Cross. Without these two cornerstones of inner healing, we may be delivered from a demon's influence; but the demon may return later with seven others worse than himself, as Jesus warned in Luke 11:24-26. We have observed that it is the Father's love in renewal that so often makes inner healing viable and receivable in our hearts.

## Spiritual Warfare

Without inner healing and transformation we may charge onto our battlefields carrying a lot of baggage from our childhood and with great gaping holes in our armor—unhealed wounds, sinful self-protection, anger, unforgiveness and so on. As Christians, we are hidden in Christ (see Col. 3:3), but in battle we are exposed. It is wisdom not to go into spiritual warfare as lone rangers. After warfare we need to pray hiding prayers.

Before entering into spiritual warfare, consider the following questions: Do you trust authority? Has the Lord called you and instructed you? Have you put all pride to death on the Cross? Can you be part of a team, part of the Lord's army? Can you listen to and follow directions? Can you accept parameters? Are you jealous of others' gifts? Do you value being tested? How do you feel about being disciplined? Do you know what it is to wait on the Lord? Are you secure in Him? Do you trust the Lord to show up? Do you trust Him to protect you? John and I recommend that you consider attending a few classes at the Toronto Airport Christian Fellowship or elsewhere. Let the Father's Blessing open you more fully to study with others. Avoid the backlash of Satan's counterattack by basking in the loving fellowship of believers, as well as abiding in the strong tower of who He is (see Prov. 18:10).

## Unity

Ephesians 2:21,22 speaks of the whole building being fitted together, growing into a dwelling place of God. Ephesians 4:3 calls us to be diligent to preserve the unity of the Spirit in the bond of peace. How powerfully this is demonstrated again and again as thousands of people from every culture, race and denominational background come together at renewal gatherings to share Christ and to build friendships. Ephesians 4:12,13 speaks of the equipping of the saints for the work of service, to the building up of the Body of Christ until we all attain to unity of faith, to a mature man. We are to speak the truth in love, to grow up into Christ, in whom the whole Body, according to the proper working of each individual part, causes growth of the Body for the building up of itself in love. Ephesians 4:22-24 says we are to lay aside the old self, put on the new self in God's likeness, and be renewed in the spirit of our mind. This is what the renewal movement and the ministry of inner healing and transformation are all about!

## Reconciliation

Reconciliation is surely what God is doing in our time—in families, among friends, between tribes and nations. This means getting to know one another. It necessitates repentance and forgiveness, the very essence of inner healing and transformation. As His love fills us, we learn to let that love flow through us to others.

## Evangelization

In John 17, Jesus prayed that we be perfected in unity so that the world may know that God sent Him. More than the sermons we preach, *we are* the message. We must be healed if we are to represent Him well. Thousands are being converted today and are asking "Now what?" Many are hanging onto the old as well as naming Christ, just to cover all their bases. We must be willing to disciple them so they can grow up in their salvation. This is happening more and more as both inner healing and renewal ministries send out teams and teaching materials all around the world.

Ed Silvoso reported to us that the Argentinian revival, now in its 17th year, *retains* 90 percent of its converts, whereas American crusades *lose* 90 percent. What accounts for this difference? In Argentina, newborn converts are immediately subjected to three days of intensive inner healing and deliverance, and a few weeks later to another three-day session in which they not only receive but are also taught how to minister to others. The Father's love undergirds and enables men and women as they are launched into the sanctification process by which Christians mature into His likeness.

# Jesus coming for a bride

Jesus is returning for *one Bride,* not a harem of brides, especially not a bunch who pick one another apart with accusation, criticism and rejection! His Bride must be a resting place for her husband. She must be a beautiful, loving unit of *one*. She is now being called to account, cleansed and prepared.

So we see in all the ways God is moving today that the Father's Blessing (via Toronto) and inner healing go together, like hand and glove, supporting and making each more fruitful. What binds us to the hurts and practices of the past is mainly fear of exposure, failure, recrimination, blame, censure, rejection. Experiencing the wonder of our Father's love for us eases away these fears, like dead old leaves floating away in the river of His love. The uniqueness of the Father's Blessing at Toronto is that His love gently flows over and past the dams of our stony hearts, washing us clean and free.

Since October 1994, wherever Paula and I go to teach and whenever our hosts will allow, we immerse people in the river of His love through the laying on of hands and prayer. It has been a never-ending joy and is still a surprise to witness how the Lord faithfully pours Himself into the hearts of His children—refreshing, revitalizing and healing them. Most fall slain in the Spirit, but they are free to receive either standing or sitting. Few manifest much in our ministry other than occasional laughter or tears. It's such a wonderful blessing to see Christians experiencing—some for the first time—the reality of His very present love. We all need His presence. When we encounter it, our faith moves from dry belief to the wonder of His reality.

What did we ever do beforehand? How did we survive? With gritted teeth and hope beyond hope for something better, I suppose. What a gift from God that we no longer have to be those who believe without putting our fingers in His side in order to exclaim, "My Lord and my God!" (John 20:28). We know Him. We love Him. And best of all, we are loved by Him—really and refreshingly, again and again.

# i see you, God

## DAVID LAZARUS

*David Lazarus has been sharing the good news about Yeshua with Jews and Arabs for over two decades. Together with his wife, Michaella, they nurture a Joshua generation of young messianic believers now arising in Israel. Their four children have record-ed original children's Hebrew worship, and together they long for the day of salvation for peoples of Israel. David pastors Beit Immanuel Congregation in Tel Aviv, Israel. I shall never forget meeting David. He came into my office soon after we had moved into our building on Attwell Drive. Several people from Israel had come to Toronto, hungry for more of God, yet David was very skeptical and full of questions. Finally, when we prayed for him, he was touched so mightily by the Lord that I wondered how he would survive! His skepticism went right out the window and he returned to Israel absolutely on fire for God. Here this servant of the Lord describes the lasting fruit of a mighty baptism in the Holy Spirit and fire. —J. A.*

*Encounters with God.* Moses encountered God on Mount Sinai at a burning bush and was transformed from a runaway, stutter-ing fugitive into the statesman-leader of God's covenant peo-ple. Paul encountered God on his way to Damascus and was transformed from a self-righteous, Christ-hating zealot to the greatest proponent of the revelation of God's grace in the Messiah.

*An encounter with God.* You can't do anything to make it happen, but when it happens, it changes everything. An encounter with God happens in a moment and will change you for an eternity. You can't buy it at any price, but having it will cost you everything.

My first encounter with God was 22 years ago on a sand dune in the Sinai Desert as the sun set over the shores of the Red Sea. I'd been living there for three years, alone, silent, fishing and trading with Bedouin tribesmen for food and matches. Trying to make some sense out of life, I sought the desert solitude because things bothered me about the world we live in: hatred, racism, war, terrorism, the Holocaust. What kind of a world could allow that to happen? What kind of people were we anyway?

Somewhere in my travels I'd picked up a Bible with the Old and New Testaments, one of those Gentile editions. Reading the words of Yeshua for the very first time left a deep impression on me. Here was truth, pure and simple. He didn't beat around the bush; He spoke straight and poignantly about life, love, values, faith. His words were honey to my lips, apples of gold. Devouring the pages of the Gospels, something strange began to happen to me. It was no longer me reading His words, but His Word was reading me. Instead of a lonely soul finding courage and meaning in the words of a great prophet, the Son of God was piercing the veil of my heart, revealing who I really was.

In a moment of time I realized that within me was the same hatred, murder, shame and horror that had so grieved me. I saw in my own heart the darkness I had so feared. The problem was not only in the world; it was here, in my own heart. I was ruined, and I prepared to walk out to the sea and end my shameful life.

That's when I had my first encounter with God. A presence, or cloudlike atmosphere, descended around me. That's the only way I know to describe it. The impact upon my senses was more real to me than the tears of despair soaking my face. This presence demanded my full attention, and immediately I knew—simply, wonderfully and fearfully knew—that Yeshua Himself had come to me.

To an inner place of my being, a place I did not even know existed, He spoke: "Now you see truth, but only in part. I am the truth that will set you free because I am forgiveness for your sin. I died on the Cross to pay for the darkness you have found in your heart."

My mind objected: *Jews don't believe in Jesus!* But my heart's longing for pardon was reaching out to receive this offer of forgiveness, and I was born again. Opening my eyes I saw a new world—God's world. The leaves of the palm trees, so green—had I never seen that before? The sea, so brilliantly blue—how had I not noticed? That encounter changed my life forever.

In 1980 a peace treaty was signed between Egypt and Israel. Egypt got the Sinai Desert and I had to leave. Imagining myself the only Jew in the world who believed in Yeshua; and sensing a call to tell my people about the Messiah, I moved to Tel-Aviv. I discovered a fellowship with other Messianic Jews—I was not the only one, after all! There I met my wife, Michaella. Gradually we were moved into leadership roles in the Beit Avinu Congregation and in a growing movement of Jews coming to faith in Yeshua.

Finding other Jewish believers was certainly a great joy, but congregational life was not quite what I had anticipated. Being in leadership exposed us to a world of jealousies and conflict, heartbreaks and disappointments. But before long we were pastoring a growing congregation that boasted inspiring sermons, anointed worship, strategic spiritual warfare, exciting outreaches, a great children's ministry and all the right doctrines on baptism, tongues and the Second Coming. You name it, we had it—or else we'd soon get it! I should also mention one other area that we excelled in—faultfinding. We had it down to a science and actually kept files on ministries with weak points and false doctrines!

The fact was our love had grown cold and any real joy we had had in the ministry was in deep freeze! We worked and worked, harder and harder, but the same old problems kept coming back in people's lives. With all of our glorious church ministry, well, it just didn't seem like we were getting anywhere. I quickly figured out what the problem was: we just were not giving it enough effort! So we poured ourselves into the ministry even more. Before long I was completely burned out; my dear wife and our four kids were completely worn out too.

It was around this time that we heard about what was happening in Toronto and it was mostly negative reports. We were told it was hype, emotionalism or the transference of some kind of hypnotic state. Most were convinced that it was a counterfeit sent to deceive even the elect. We were so worn out and discouraged, however, that we figured we had nothing to lose by going to investigate it.

We made the trip to Toronto, like so many others, and waited hours in the freezing Canadian rain to get into a cramped little church. Standing there shivering in the line, you could tell the newcomers from those who'd already been there awhile. We newcomers were desperate but didn't want anybody to know. The others were desperate and seemed happy about it!

By the second day, I thought I was foolish to have come to Toronto. The worship was good, but hey, I'd seen better. The preaching was, well, interesting, when the preacher wasn't under God's power or when you could hear what he was saying over the laughter. This one lady next to us sounded like she was about to deliver a baby right there in her seat! I just tuned out of the service and said to God and to myself, *Lord, I don't need this. I'm tired; let's go home. This was not what I had in mind when I said I needed to be refreshed. But since I've come all this way and spent all that money, I might as well spend some time with*

*You while I'm here.* That's when I had my second encounter with God.

I hesitate to describe the actual feelings or sensations of this encounter. When Scripture describes encounters people have with God, not much is said about what they felt. Acts 10:10 simply says that Peter "fell into a trance"; and in Acts 9, Paul saw a light flash from heaven, fell down and was left blind for three days. We are told few details of the experiences themselves. Scripture emphasizes the results—what changed in the person's life. In the case of Peter, a vision he saw three times opened his heart to meet with the Gentile Cornelius and ultimately led to the early believers' accepting Gentiles into their fellowship (see Acts 15). For Paul, his was a conversion experience of such impact that he became the leading apostle to the nations. Amazing things happen when men encounter God.

In my own situation, suffice it to say that as I took my eyes off of what was happening around me and looked to the Lord, a weight or presence engulfed me. This time, however, it was so intense that I was literally pinned to the floor. It was strong, yet gentle; heavy, yet tender, like being fastened to the floor by a million tons of rose petals, and God was in the midst of them. For four days after that, day and night, I encountered God as my Father. I couldn't walk or sleep, and I hardly ate; friends carried me back and forth between the hotel and the meetings.

This encounter transformed my life and continues to affect my family and our congregation. I discovered that all my efforts to please Him were totally unnecessary. This surprised me. I honestly believed that God was, at least in some measure, pleased with my hard work. God showed me that He is pleased with us because we are His children and not because of what we do. I saw that in heaven much of what we think we have done for the Kingdom will be forgotten, and much that we've forgotten will be remembered.

God also showed me that I had been living with the fear of man in my heart for many years. Much of my behavior, ways of thinking and relating, even my personality were often the result of seeking acceptance from friends. I began to realize that this fear had prevented me from maturing properly as a pastor. The constant need to please people had crippled the development of my gifts and personality. I think in some ways I already suspected that I might be satisfying my ego needs through the ministry; I just never knew what to do about it. But now, in His wonderful presence, it was as simple as asking my Father, "Would You set me free?" Somehow I understood that was the very reason I was on the floor encountering Him.

Friends often say to me now, "David, you've changed. We're not so sure about Toronto and that experience you had, but you sure are different. You're a much nicer guy!" Not really. I have changed some, but I think what is really happening is that they are seeing the real David for the first time! I no longer need to hide behind fears or try to be something I'm not.

In Deuteronomy 1:26-31 (*NIV*), the children of Israel were "unwilling to go up" because they were afraid. They claimed "our brothers have made us lose heart" (vs. 28). They were more concerned with the opinions of man than with the heart of God. That's why the Lord spoke to them through Moses and said,

Do not be terrified; do not be afraid of them. The LORD your God, who is going before you, will fight for you, as he did for you in Egypt . . . and in the desert. There you saw how *the LORD your God carried you, as a father carries his son*, all the way you went until you reached this place (vv. 29-31, emphasis added).

God was teaching Israel that He was their Father so that they would not fear. One of the most important roles of a father is to teach his children not to be afraid. A child who grows up in the security of a father's care is able to gain the confidence he needs to take on challenges and try new things. A good father will not only protect his children but will also instill within them the confidence they need to stand up for themselves.

Knowing God as our Father means having the confidence to do the things He is calling us to do without fear. Even Yeshua's call began with the affirmation, "You are My beloved Son; in You I am well pleased" (Luke 3:22, *NKJV*). This was at the very beginning of His ministry, before He had done anything. This affirmation must precede anything we do for God. Ministry begins when a child of God, secure in the Father's love, can step out with courage in obedience to His commands.

Confidence is knowing that someone is going to be there to pick you up when you fall. Confidence is an ability to trust—an inner security that allows you to step out and try new things, knowing that you may even fall a few times, but it doesn't matter. You're learning to walk. The word "confidence" means with faith. To have confidence is to know that you can step out and become what you are meant to be because there is somebody watching over you, someone who cares.

A father also provides an atmosphere of love, grace and gentleness where a child's unique personality and character can develop without shame or harsh correction. Today I would rather submit to the simple work God is doing in my life and in our congregation than try to reproduce what others are doing elsewhere. In the past, I was so afraid of failure that I'd copy other pastors' styles, use someone else's sermon or try and replicate another person's ministry. Now my own ways of serving are developing. They may not be as profound or great as someone else's, but they produce better fruit. Out of my own simple Father-son relationship with God, He is using me to set others free and to pastor people in a way that's making a difference. I enjoy ministry now in a way I never could before.

As I have become more confident in my relationship with the Lord, I am far more willing and able to release others into their calling and gifts. I have seen people (who never would have considered themselves capable) released into their callings because they feel safe and loved. The people in our fellowship are more confident because the pastor is not so uptight and nervous! Where relationships once made me anxious and exhausted, I've now learned how God brings us relationships as a source of joy and encouragement, not to wear us out.

A great result from this newfound freedom is seen in the birth of a team of lay leaders for my church. For years I had prayed that the Lord would raise up such a team to help carry the responsibility of overseeing the congregation's life. Sadly, no team ever developed before my encounter with the Father at Toronto. Why? Because up to that point I was wracked with personal fears and insecurity—afraid to release the younger men and women for service. Only as my heart changed and became infused with confidence from God was that team allowed to become a reality. Today we walk in accountability and vulnerability; we pray together and share responsibility for the daily oversight of the flock.

I was so glad when John Arnott titled his first book on the renewal *The Father's Blessing*. That is exactly what it has been for us: our Father's Blessing as He comes to His children in many ways and many forms, imparting to us all that we require to lead fruitful lives.

When we first came home to our congregation after Toronto, we were so on fire. We just knew that we had tapped into the most wonderful blessing our Father could give, His Holy Spirit, and that He would bring refreshment, joy and hope to our people. Were we surprised when some of our people refused to even listen to what the Lord was doing in our lives! Rumors, gossip and contention spread quickly and our membership dropped to only a few. But God has been so faithful to us. He has rebuilt our congregation into a whole new family, much larger than we ever were before and much happier too.

We are growing in the personal knowledge and experience of God as our Father! I've never understood why some cannot acknowledge this as a wonderful blessing from the Father—one of the most glorious and important moves of God in recent Church history. Nevertheless, it's not too late to enter in. We say, "More, Lord! More!"

# further up and further in

## JOSEPH L. GARLINGTON, SR.

*Joseph Garlington, senior pastor of Covenant Church in Pittsburgh, Pennsylvania, is well known for his teaching and ministry of reconciliation and also for leading worship at national Promise Keepers events. A few years ago, Carol and I agreed to do meetings at a hotel in Pittsburgh, and there we met Joseph, one of the pastors supporting our meetings in that city. When we went out for dinner later, Carol recognized him as someone who had been to our meetings in Toronto. He had come to check us out and had gotten as close as he could by catching for my wife as she ministered to the people. He shares his amazing testimony of how God met him powerfully and personally. —J. A.*

Today, I believe that the great tragedy of the Pentecostal-Charismatic-Third Wave expression is its capitulation to the criticisms of those who have never had such an encounter and yet have become authorities on how such an encounter should look if there actually were such things today! This surrender has produced an uneasy awkwardness among those of us who desire the Holy Spirit to do all that He wants in us and in His Church. We are torn between the two poles of pseudolegitimacy in matters theological and in the authentic work that has actually taken place in our lives as a result of our wholehearted embracing of this fresh work of the Spirit.

I came to Toronto because "the Spirit bade me go." I like to say that I was "incrediblized" by what I saw and experienced. To be honest, at first I was deeply irritated. I saw people responding to the Holy Spirit's presence in a way that was eerily like déjà vu.

I was provoked, frustrated and angered that suddenly—because middle-class, professional and mainline denominational people were shaking and jerking—this had *now* become a legitimate expression of God's power. All my life I had heard critics and detractors call these same things emotionalism, fleshly and, later, soulish; so I resolved to avoid them in my desperate pursuit for acceptance by conservative Christians.

Thirty years later, I found myself in Toronto, Canada, in the dead of winter, and something was slowly boiling inside me. I looked at my roots and fought a multitude of emotions. I simultaneously battled resentment and loss—loss because for years I had despised my heritage, and resentment because somehow I had been forced to abandon my heritage in order to be considered legitimate. I was building up a real head of steam, when suddenly the Holy Spirit brought peace to me. It was as though He was saying, "Joseph, don't worry about the past. Just enjoy Me, and let the past go." A friend of mine with a similar background experienced a similar thing and said the Holy Spirit told him, "Don't be like the elder brother. Just enjoy the party."

The next few days were transforming. I have been in ministry since I was 14 years old, and I was trained how to give but not how to receive. I remember once being admonished by one of John Wimber's leaders that I had a difficult time receiving. I didn't know what he meant at that time, nor did I know how to do it even if I wanted to; but in those early days at TACF, I became very adept at receiving.

TACF leaders exhorted us not to pray for anyone but just to receive ourselves. When you are addicted to ministry and it's time to pray for people, I know some guys who could come out of the grave to do that! My wife, Barbara, and I and most of our leaders spent a lot of time receiving—and we actually began to look forward to the prayer times.

Our first pleasant discovery during the ministry times was that almost *anyone* on the ministry teams was effective at ministering to us. At first, we would look for the power pray-ers—the ones who seemed to be the most effective in personal ministry. We would run forward and jockey for a good spot, hoping one of the power pray-ers would come in our direction. We soon found out, however, that most of the team members were effective in ministering and releasing the work of the Holy Spirit in any one of us.

One of the significant memorials of my life occurred during one of the morning intercessory prayer times. One morning during corporate intercession, one of TACF's pastors, Ian Ross, led prayer and said he sensed that the pastors who were present should release their churches and ministries to the Lord.

Now having done this on *many* prior occasions in my ministry, I felt no real need to do it again. However, I went forward out of modesty and courtesy and with the encouragement of my senior associate, thinking, *What do I have to lose by doing it again?* The prayer time that followed was revelatory and it became blatantly clear to me that I had regained another frantic chokehold on the ministry—and for some reason known only to God, I was desperately holding on to it.

After the prayer time, some of our intercessors shared with me their observations. Two of them had discerned that a very deep spiritual struggle was going on in me during that time of intercession. They had begun to intercede as Ian patiently continued praying for me. Even later, my son-in-law Michael confirmed how real the warfare was to him as he prayed. It seemed like a long time, but I knew exactly the moment of surrender and I knew who had won the battle for His church! Several months later I could see the precious fruit of that surrender; our church and my ministry have never been the same.

After five glorious days in God's presence, our team returned to Pittsburgh—empowered, refreshed and invigorated for a coming year of ministry that would be one of the most exciting in our church history and life. The entire congregation of Covenant Church knew that we had had an encounter with God. They could see it on our countenances and they wanted some of what they saw in us. We all shared freely as it became abundantly clear that the Holy Spirit would meet hungry people wherever they are.

# times of refreshing

Our church is not unaccustomed to great moments in worship. I have taught and written on worship for many years, and more than any other subject, it is my primary passion. We have had worship services where we were swept gloriously into the very presence of God, and we just stayed there. We are accustomed to strangers visiting our services and simply weeping the entire time, without knowing why. The presence of God is not an unfamiliar thing among us. But these new days were accompanied by a greater intensity in worship, a deeper desire to be broken for Him, and a total absence of self-consciousness in our worship and our worship postures. This was worship heightened to a degree that we had not previously known. Since that time, one of my definitions of worship is to move from self-consciousness to God-consciousness.

These times of refreshing were awesome. People were hungry and desperate for God, and we ministered to everyone the way ministry was modeled at TACF. There are persons now in ministry in our church whose lives were powerfully and radically changed just from the overflow of our days in Toronto. The ongoing legacy of these refreshing times at Covenant is multi-fold. We have come to a greater dependency upon the Holy Spirit to accomplish the Father's work. We have come to a deeper sensitivity to the Holy Spirit's moving in our services. We have come to a place of comfort about the way *He* chooses to manifest Himself in our midst. Our ministry styles are less dependent upon hype and more dependent upon His power to accomplish the work. Jesus said that He cast out evil spirits by the finger of God or by the power of the Holy Spirit; God's finger is far more powerful than any resource we have for ministry.

I returned to Toronto in January 1995, in the midst of our times of refreshing. Ironically, I didn't realize how dry I was nor the degree of my thirst for God. Barbara and I had just moved into a new home, we were making some needed additions, and I had become stressed by all of the activity that was taking place. I knew I *had* to get away. At that time, the only refuge for me was Toronto. I came alone because I wanted the solitude of a quasi-retreat, but I also needed the powerful dimension of the spiritual atmosphere of renewal that I had encountered that previous December. I was not disappointed.

Once again, the Holy Spirit was manifestly present. Sometimes I would just sit quietly in my seat and wait upon Him, and other times I would simply lie prostrate on the floor. I would often assume this posture in the privacy of my study—the only place where I had no sense of self-consciousness. But this was not my study; this was a room filled with hundreds of passionate worshipers. I quickly learned that at TACF you needn't fear disturbing anyone by your devotions. Most of the persons present seemed to be very comfortable with the various postures of worship and waiting.

In each service, I heard powerful testimonies of the Holy Spirit's work in the lives of many believers from all over the world. One by one, those stories of the Father's love began to work in me a new hope. I heard what the Father was doing in the lives of His children everywhere and I became aware of a deep and visceral hunger in my heart for *all* that the Father had for me. For the first time in my life, I wanted *Him* more than I wanted to *do* something for Him.

Some of my friends like to paraphrase Ephesians 6:7,8 this way: "Whatever good you do for others, God will make happen for you." I really do believe in this principle and I began to seek to be a servant to others who were seeking a fresh touch from God. And so, after a few days of ministry, I decided to help Carol Arnott as she was ministering to others. Carol pastors with her husband, John, TACF's senior pastor, and she is a gentle and yet powerful instrument of the Holy Spirit. I volunteered to catch for her. I learned a long time ago that more is caught than taught (no pun intended), and I closely watched and attentively listened to this incredible woman of God as she ministered the Father's love with amazing power. I observed everything she did. I even intently watched to see if she pushed or pressured people into falling. The fact is, she resisted any effort on her part to activate or instigate a spiritual event. Carol's gift of discernment of the various needs and situations in people was absolutely uncanny, and on many occasions I often would have the same witness as she ministered to someone.

Carol was like a midwife helping to bring forth the work God was already doing in the lives of those to whom she ministered. I watched, observed, learned and applied what I saw her do. Later, when I was invited to share in praying for others, I was delighted to see the Holy Spirit move with the same effectiveness and power.

Almost always when Carol finished praying for others, I would ask her to pray for me. I invariably experienced a new measure of the Holy Spirit's power flowing into my life as she gently laid her hands upon my head and chest.

More than five years later, it's difficult for me to share what happened during one of those moments without sensing my heavenly Father's infinite love for me. As Carol prayed for me, I began to weep uncontrollably—a deep, sobbing that expressed brokenness of heart. It was as though pent-up emotions, restrained for years, had found a safe and legitimate place to express themselves. It was a fountain that seemed to be waiting for some moment of vulnerability, some crack in the dike of my outward imperviousness to hurts never resolved.

Genesis 7:11 says, "In the six hundredth year of Noah's life, in the second month, on the seventeenth day of the month, on the same day all the fountains of the great deep burst open, and the floodgates of the sky were opened." In January 1995, the floodgates of my great deeps were opened. As I lay there on the floor, weeping and feeling very much out of control and very unlike an apostolic leader in the Body of Christ, I heard Carol pray, "Oh, Father, please come and touch the deep places of rejection in this man's heart."

When I heard those words, I reacted inwardly, saying in my heart, "I don't have rejection. She doesn't know who I am. I'm a respected leader in the body of Christ. I've been in successful ministry for years!"

In that moment I heard the deep and filling voice of my heavenly Father say, "You can either accept *My* view of who you are or *your* view of who you are. If you accept *My* view, I can heal you." In that moment, I submitted to Carol's discernment through the Holy Spirit and almost instantly "the fountains of the great deep" sho' 'nuff broke open! I began sobbing uncontrollably. Carol continued ministering to me in her own gentle way as she prayed that the Father would heal my broken heart.

When she sensed that her part was done, she left and I remained on the floor conscious only of His healing presence.

When I was finally able to rise, I was one of the few persons left in the room that night. I returned to my hotel worshiping and weeping. I went to sleep with a deep abiding sense that the Father had taken charge of some real old business and freed me to move on to a new arena of ministry.

The following morning, the ministry focus was pastors and leaders, and I returned to TACF with a heightened sense of anticipation for what my Father had in store. During that service, Ian called for all of us in full-time ministry to come forward and receive prayer. One of the fresh paradigms we came to see at TACF was that you could come as much as you liked and receive as much as you wanted. The psalmist blessed the Lord who daily loads us with benefits (see Ps. 103:2), and I became very comfortable with receiving prayer on a regular basis. Ian's appeal must have touched more than me because suddenly I was surrounded by about 150 other hungry pastors and leaders, many accompanied by their spouses.

As soon as Ian laid his hands on me, I sensed the same powerful presence I felt the night before and strong hands gently lowered me to the floor. Once again I began to weep as before. As I did, I felt a gentle hand on my head and I heard Carol's familiar voice saying these words: "Oh, Father, I don't know what You are doing in this precious man's life; but I ask You to continue to heal his broken heart."

I experienced the style of prayer ministry that TACF modeled: soaking. This is a regular and consistent appeal to the Holy Spirit to continue the deep work of healing in the lives of those receiving ministry. I no longer had any need to resist Carol's words. This time I willingly submitted to all that He was doing in me and I just stayed on the floor, soaking.

To this very day, I am still drawing from the deep well of healing I received that winter. It is amazing how patient the Father is in His work in our lives. I only wish that what took place in January 1995 had taken place 25 years earlier in my life and ministry.

# crybabies

The psalmist said, "My times are in your hands" (Ps. 31:15, *NIV*). The ability to recognize the times of visitations makes all the difference in seeing the Messiah in our circumstances or missing Him—even while we are looking at Him. These times are called *kairos* moments or, as *The Amplified Bible* calls them, a "critical niche in time" (Acts 1:7). Some of my associates question the validity of allowing experience to determine the genuineness of an event, but it seems to me that without authentic experiences that parallel those in the Scriptures, we have no way of truly knowing if they're real. The psalmist exhorts us to "taste and see that the LORD is good" (Ps. 34:8).

When I was growing up, sometime during my preteen years I became aware that the grown-ups in our family considered me to be a crybaby. It became a mantra from young and old, and although I couldn't see it then, I began to harden myself to those words and resisted any expressions of emotion. During my early days at Toronto, however, it seemed as though all the pent-up frustrations from early childhood on found a release. There is a tremendous parallel in the Spirit realm to the verse from Genesis 7:11 that I quoted earlier. When the "fountains of [my] great deep burst open," so also did the "floodgates of the sky."

I no longer fear the embarrassment of brokenness in public; rather, I embrace it. I now have an increasing expectation that brokenness will often precede breakthrough. In fact, I like to say "No weeping, no reaping." I have seen the Holy Spirit powerfully move in my life through intense and deep weeping as I pray for people. I believe that the enemy wanted to use childhood wounds to barricade the door to this kind of ministry.

So now I'm a crybaby again and I now proudly pastor a crybaby church. We regularly weep for the lost in early morning prayer; it is not unusual to see copious tears in the midst of a normal worship service. The apostle Paul said, "God has chosen the weak things of the world to shame the things which are strong" (1 Cor. 1:27).

I recently read a book on leadership by Margaret Wheatley called *Leadership and the New Science: Discovering Order in a Chaotic World*. As she described the "new science" and its relationship to organizations, I was struck by some of her insights into the world of quantum. And as I read her conclusions, I was amazed how much of her *previous* understanding of things had to change as the result of new revelations through the new science. Ms. Wheatley identified these conclusions as "My Growing Sensitivity to the Quantum World." What she shared powerfully summarizes my own approach to this wonderful new paradigm for ministry:

1.  I struggle to remain aware of the system as a system and give up well-trained abilities to reduce and separate things as the route to understanding.
2.  I concentrate much more on processes now, focusing on qualities rather than quantities.
3.  I pay more attention to things like patterns, direction, feel and internal rhythm.
4.  I don't personally spend time anymore on elaborate plans or time lines.

5. I believe great things are possible when we increase participation.

6. I no longer argue about what is real.[1]

She concludes these observations with this very remarkable statement: "I have given up trying to control anything—I finally understand that the universe refuses to cooperate with my desire to play God."[2]

Today the scientific world is far more open than ever to the possibility of worlds that exist beyond our previous realms of understanding. We live in a world that changes daily, and the gospel of the twenty-first century must be as powerful as it was in the first century: It is *the* power of God. A supernatural gospel preached without supernatural attestations will be simply ignored by a postmodern generation.

These incredible insights have been powerful instigators to my continuing pursuit of the presence of God. I am satisfied that if the world of quantum—a world created by God—is filled with paradoxes and inexplicable reasons for incredible phenomena, how much more the world of the Spirit? I believe we are beginning to enjoy in some small way "the glorious liberty of the children of God" (Rom. 8:21, *NKJV*).

I can honestly say that the past years have been remarkably instructive as I've returned to a childlike stance of allowing my Father to instruct me in His ways. I am convinced that there is so much more that He has for us, and the stewardship of the more requires faithfulness to what He is presently entrusting to us. I am learning to appreciate the phrase from C. S. Lewis's *Chronicles of Narnia*: "Further up, further in."

I'm aware of the human tendency to make the part the whole, and I've become sensitive to the reality that one taste is simply that—one taste—but it's not enough. I believe these wonderful experiences are simply precursors to the more that the Father has for us. While I shall not dwell upon the experiences in isolation, I rejoice that the Father has mightily used them to lead us further up and further in.

### Notes

1. Margaret J. Wheatley, *Leadership and the New Science: Discovering Order in a Chaotic World* (San Francisco: Berrett-Koehler Publishers, 1999), n.p.
2. Ibid.

# the river is here

## MAX LEGG

*In July 1995, we made our first trip to Auckland, New Zealand. Max Legg, pastor of Victory Christian Church in Auckland, had gone out on a limb during a critical situation for us and invited us over for meetings in his very hungry nation. The church was packed, the overflow area was full, and God moved in incredible power. I believe that nation is still reeling from the impact of those meetings. —J. A.*

*There is a river whose streams make glad the city of God, the holy place where the Most High dwells. God is within her, she will not fall; God will help her at break of day (Ps. 46: 4,5, NIV).*

In the early 1920s, Smith Wigglesworth visited Wellington, New Zealand. The resulting move of God greatly impacted our country. In 1927, the First Assembly of God Church was established in Auckland. Today it is known as Victory Christian Church.

In 1970, the church was mightily blessed by the charismatic movement, and the congregation grew from 50 to 3,000 in just a few years, becoming the largest church in Australasia. It was a church known around the world for its great worship, teaching and vision for missions.

My wife, Beverly, and I were born again and filled with the Spirit during this revival. Week by week people flooded to the altar and their lives were changed radically. This move of God was quite similar to what is currently happening in Pensacola.

At its zenith in the early '80s, the church suffered a major upheaval with the resignation of their dearly loved pastor. The fallout was catastrophic and the congregation diminished significantly. At this time, the church was committed to the construction of a 4,000-seat auditorium but with rampant inflation, rising interest rates and a continuing decline in membership, this vision became a huge financial burden. The building was to have been finished by 1984 at a cost of $4 million, but by 1987 the church was $8 million in debt. I believe the church was in captivity in the 1980s as God purged deeply rooted sin and tested the congregation's commitment to the vision. The church had bought five acres of land in midcity Auckland. It is a very visible property in a strategic location; as a result, it was greatly sought after by others. We purchased the property half an hour before the Moslems made a bid to build a mosque there.

After an intense four years on staff as associate pastor, I became senior pastor in mid-1993. On the day of my induction, I received a fax from our lenders, requesting an immediate sale of the property and repayment of the loan. In August 1994, we received a demand letter followed by a foreclosure notice to take effect on April 12, 1995. It felt like the Lord had put me in a leadership position with a guillotine over my head!

The congregation that had carried the burden of the church for 10 years was becoming very weary; many were hurt and angry. Over a period of four years, beginning in 1989, the people had given very sacrificially; and with God's intervention the debt was reduced to $3 million by 1994. The faithful 10 percent of the original congregation of 3,000 people still held to God's vision and purpose for the church.

At the same time the foreclosure notice hit my desk in September 1994, God visited the church in an exceptional way during a Sunday morning service. The Holy Spirit fell on the congregation and many people fell to the floor and began to roar with laughter. All over the auditorium, people began to cry out in high praise. Some were lying prostrate on the floor; others worshiped, jumped, danced or shook. A month prior to this visitation, I had heard of meetings in other parts of New Zealand where people were rolling around the floor laughing, not able to walk to the altar or even to their cars. I'd heard that these meetings ran late into the night and I remembered back to 1993 when God had visited our church primary school in a similar way. The children and their teachers were radically transformed.

I began to inquire further about what was taking place and eventually called in a pastor who had experienced this fresh outpouring. He prayed for me and I shot across the room, hitting the wall with a thud. *What on earth was this?* I thought. I became intoxicated in the Holy Spirit and then started praying for my leaders. They began to fall all over the floor! We had experienced falling to the ground previously under the anointing of the Holy Spirit but never as powerfully as this. I asked the Lord to show me from His Word what was happening, and Psalm 126 came to my mind. I then realized that God was bringing the church out of captivity.

There was much joy, dancing and vibrant worship, and many in the congregation had a refired passion for Jesus. In many services I could not stand because of the weight of God's presence. My wife and I and many others fell to the floor laughing and often stayed there the whole service. We had been through a desert experience and now our heavenly Father was giving us a much-needed drink. Isaiah 32:15 (*NIV*) was being fulfilled among us: "the Spirit is poured upon us from on high, and the desert becomes a fertile field, and the fertile field seems like a forest."

In October 1994, I read an article in the *Zealandia*, a New Zealand Catholic magazine, about six priests who went to the Toronto Airport Church and were touched by God in an unusual way. The title of the article was "Ha, Ha, He, He, Haw, Haw, Ho, Ho, Ho." Their story lined up with what we had experienced. My wife and I heard the Lord encouraging us to go to Toronto to learn how to flow in this wonderful, refreshing outpouring of the Holy Spirit.

On December 12, 1994, we arrived to find things exactly as the six Catholic priests had said. Thirsty and hungry Christians from all over the world were there getting full of the Holy Spirit and giving testimony of how God had revived them from exhaustion, breakdown and burnout. It was beautiful to see how, in a few hours and days, people's lives were being turned around by God. Many pastors and church members who had been deeply hurt were receiving healing in their emotions. For that whole week, Beverly and I stayed at the evening meetings until well after midnight. These services were something out of the ordinary.

During that week, church historian Guy Chevreau gave wonderful teaching to the pastors about what was happening among us. I bought his book *Catch the Fire*, which explained from Scripture and from records of past revivals what was currently taking place around the world. The things we were seeing in our church and in Toronto had indeed been noted in previous revivals.

On our last night at Toronto, things went a little quiet around 10:00 P.M. Then the worship leader began to sing "The River Is Here." Immediately the whole congregation burst into dance. It went on for hours until we were all worn out. I believed that song was prophetic for New Zealand, so I brought the music back to our church. The song went through the nation like a prophetic trumpet.

After arriving home in Auckland, I wrote to John and Carol, inviting them to New Zealand. They accepted our invitation and gave June 20, 1995, as their date of arrival. We were only four months away from facing a mortgagee sale, with the likelihood of losing our $12 million investment. Inviting the Arnotts was a test of my faith because the impending mortgage auction sale was scheduled for April 12. I shared this with the congregation; we knew we needed a huge miracle.

We prayed fervently about what to do. Should we sell the building and relocate, as many church leaders had advised us, or hold on in faith to the vision God had given our church way back in 1978? We researched all the prophetic words of the past and waged urgent warfare over them, as it says to do in 1 Timothy 1:18. In the midst of all this prayer, God spoke a fresh word to us about flowing in His river. Both Psalm 46:4,5 and Revelation 22:3 indicated clearly that God wanted us to stay in the river where curses break off and healing flows. Although we were under phenomenal pressure, we knew that the Holy Spirit was leading us.

I wrote to 2,500 churches in New Zealand, from the top of the North Island to the bottom of the South Island, telling them of our plight and that there was a possibility of our losing all. The market value of the land at that time was very low and every week, for some time, we were receiving offers of from $3 to $3.5 million. We had many offers from property developers around the city and even from some large religious sects.

The evening before the auction, with no real solution to our predicament, we gathered together in the auditorium for a prayer meeting. I will never forget that night. The people rose up in faith and praised God with all their strength, thanking Him for His delivering power. The river of joy was flowing! Although for five months we had seen the huge mortgage sale signs up on our property and prospective buyers wandering around our building, the congregation still believed that God would deliver us, even at this late hour. I received many encouraging messages from churches all over New Zealand.

God had told us in Psalm 46:5 that at the break of day He would help us. This is precisely what He did. At 7:00 A.M. on the day of the auction, a businessman of excellent repute and who knew of our plight called our lawyers, his lawyer and the mortgagee's lawyer to work through our situation. Our church office was like a war office all morning. By 1:30 we realized we needed more time. The auctioneers agreed to give us one more hour: at 3:00 P.M. the sale would proceed, no matter what. At 2:59, we received a fax from our mortgagee accepting our offer. We had less than one minute to notify the real estate auction room to halt the sale! We were numb, amazed and tired. God had proven again that He is a mighty deliverer of His people. That afternoon I was visited by someone from television station TVNZ, asking for a news report, which was broadcast nationwide that evening. This report brought tremendous joy to the hearts of those who had stood with us in prayer and financial support. The faith of many, many people had been greatly rewarded.

A wonderful thing happened the following Monday morning. Fifty of our primary school children filed into my office with a big thank-you card. They thanked me for trusting God and leading the church in faith to believe that He would help us. These children, I discovered later, had been coming up to the auditorium every day, standing around the huge pillars and asking God to save the building. They saw their prayers answered with a wonderful miracle.

In preparation for the arrival of John and Carol Arnott, we wrote to every church across New Zealand that had supported us, inviting them personally to the Catch the Fire conference. We organized a video link across the harbor to another Assembly of God church to cope with the crowds. We had approximately

3,000 people per meeting, twice daily for four days. It was wonderful to meet John and Carol for the first time, and the conference was outstanding. God's presence filled the house; bodies fell to the floor all around us; and others were laughing, crying, jumping for joy, jerking, running or rolling. My associate and I were supposed to lead the meetings, but neither of us was in any state even to take the offering, so others had to step in!

In the 1970s, our church had been very exclusive, the only place to be. Now it was filled with all denominations—Catholics, Anglicans, Presbyterians, Baptists, Methodists, Independents, New Lifers, Assemblies of God, Brethren, Apostolic, Vineyard, Salvation Army—they were all there!

In every meeting I was experiencing thunderbolts from the Holy Spirit. Many people I prayed for wept intensely for 15 minutes; then with a great sigh the burdens they had carried would lift off them and they would break out into laughter. God was healing and liberating those who had experienced very little freedom in their Christian life. A South African man ran down the aisle at one of the meetings and fell over on the way, bursting with laughter. He testified that in his culture it is not acceptable for a man to show emotion or to express love. Crying in front of others, especially your wife and children, was considered a sign of weakness. He said that in all his 23 years of marriage, he had never told his wife he loved her and he hadn't shown any affection to his children. As a result of what God was doing in his life at these meetings, he phoned home to his wife and children and told them he loved them. He also told them that he couldn't wait to get home to tell them again and to hug them. His family couldn't believe what they were hearing!

I'll never forget the last Catch the Fire meeting. A rather large lady, who was beside herself with laughter, was rolling backwards and forwards across our foyer, over the top of the people lying around her! Her laughter was so infectious that those around her began to roar with joy. John got this woman up to testify. She had received healing from terrible abuse in her childhood.

In October 1996, John and Carol returned to Auckland for three nights and then decided to return in February and March 1997 for a 40 Days Ablaze conference. Twelve inner-city churches shared in the running of these meetings and another 96 Auckland churches supported the conference. John and Carol ministered during the first two weeks and John Freel, Curtis Hinds, Barry Boucher and Wesley Campbell shared the remaining weeks. We saw 630 decisions for Christ at those meetings.

During 1995 and 1996, I had two major heart attacks and had undergone triple bypass surgery, two angiograms and an angioplasty. Slight heart attacks register an enzyme count of 350, but my first heart attack in 1995 registered 7,000! The doctor had to use electric shock four times to revive me. The next morning the entire emergency staff came to intensive care to see with their own eyes that I was still alive! Once again God came through and delivered me from premature death.

Not only did I have heart problems, but my administrator did too. Maurice had serious angina. This greatly burdened John and Carol and they e-mailed home asking their intercessors to pray. They researched a little about the history of our church and then took the matter to God. The Holy Spirit revealed that our church had caused great hurt and offense to the Body of Christ in New Zealand in the late 1970s and early 1980s.

With John's help, our eldership wrote up a statement to be read as a public confession and apology. We set the next Wednesday night as the reconciliation night. The auditorium was packed out. We stood, very nervously, before this huge crowd. As an eldership we apologized for all the hurts and offenses our church had caused over the years. Forty pastors of different denominations ran down to the front to meet us and hugged us all so tightly. We wept and wept and wept. God broke a very strong yoke over our fellowship, and an amazing healing took place in the Auckland churches.

If you were to ask me what this powerful move of God has done in my life and ministry to this point, I would say that I now have a far greater fire of passion for Jesus. Prophecy, visions and dreams have come to me in increasing measure and with great clarity. The gifts of the Holy Spirit are functioning in my life more effectively and I'm praying that they will increase. I am moving in a far greater degree of the power of the Holy Spirit to minister healing and deliverance. I have an increasing hunger to study the Word of God, and I have a special appreciation and love for Christians across the denominations.

Before renewal came, I was running the church and calling the Holy Spirit up to help me when I needed Him. It was a bit like the queen of England calling up the duke on odd occasions! I know in my heart God has come by His Holy Spirit to take back His Church. He is God. We need to submit to Him and let Him lead and direct His Church.

Considering our situation as a church, I believe that if the Holy Spirit hadn't come like He did, we would never have made it through in one piece. The pressure was relentless and we needed that river desperately. The devil tried to destroy our church and to kill me. He failed because we came to the river of life and stayed there. I believe that healing will come to our nation only as we flow in the river and experience the life it brings. The cost is high, but in the end there is no joy in the world like the joy in the Holy Spirit.

# out of heaven

## ADRIAN GRAY

*For 25 years, Adrian Gray has pastored Christian Life Center Mount Annan in Sydney, Australia. I first met Adrian in Sunderland, England. He was attending a conference we were doing there with Ken and Lois Gott. Adrian was keen for revival and hot after God. He has continued to seek hard after the Lord's presence and continues to host meetings at his church, which has become a revival center where the Holy Spirit has touched many hundreds of thousands of lives. Listen as he tells us of God's amazing work there. —J. A.*

The events at Toronto Airport Christian fellowship were a "touchpaper," rekindling the smoldering flames of revival that already existed in my heart. I had been born again in 1963 with a similar revival-type spirit.

In June 1963, following two years of prayer and fasting, the church in which I was saved invited an itinerant evangelist to their small community of believers and experienced a six-week revival, during which time salvations, signs, wonders, miracles and healings occurred.

I am a direct product of that Holy Ghost outpouring. This six-week encounter radically changed my life, imparting a taste for God that has never left me. As a 17-year-old, and only days after my conversion, I was evangelizing on the streets of my city. I burned with a passion for souls and for revival and was imbued with a spirit of faith.

How do we capture and retain this and future outpourings of God's Holy Spirit? Why, when many churches and fellowships were touched, did only a few seem to retain what was imparted? The import of what has occurred at Christian Life Centre Mount Annan, Sydney, Australia, may hold some keys to capturing and retaining future outpourings.

# the 1994 visitation

There have been significant steps along the way to the outpouring of the Father's Blessing. In February 1986, while attending a Pentecostal ministers' conference at which Bob Mumford was the speaker, there was a very strong prophetic word that came directly from heaven to our hearts. Malachi 3:1, "The Lord, whom you seek, will suddenly come to His temple." We knew that this was a promise from God that He would indeed visit us with His presence. Many times during the next eight years, my wife, Kathy, and I would call out to God and remind Him of His promise. "Lord, You said You would come to Your Temple. When are You going to come?" On the first weekend of November 1994, God came and we knew without a doubt that this was what He had promised.

In January 1993, we had just concluded 10 days of prayer and fasting. Another pastor and I had spent the whole 10 days in our prayer chapel waiting on the Lord. Every day and through every night we were joined by dozens of church members as we sought God for the coming year and for revival to come to our city. Our church has large overhead power transmission lines traversing the length of the property. Regular maintenance helicopter patrols take place for the Energy Commission. On the morning after we concluded the 10 days of prayer, one of these patrols reported that he had seen the church building being consumed by fire. Thirteen fire engines suddenly arrived in our car park, only to find at the deserted church building no fire to extinguish. It was the fire of God! What an outstanding prophetic sign! The church was in awe. God was up to something, but what?

In January 1994, the city of Sydney was ringed by incredible bushfires. One of Australia's foremost prophets prophesied that as the city had been surrounded by natural fire, it would also be surrounded by the fire of God. The first weekend of November 1994, a sovereign move of God descended out of heaven to the church at Mount Annan. On that same weekend, several other churches in Sydney were similarly visited, surrounding the city with the fire of God.

For many months the church had been crying out for a visitation of God. On that first weekend an evangelist had been invited to spearhead a campaign with an end-time emphasis. He had recently returned from Toronto. At the conclusion he called for those who wanted a fresh touch from God to step forward. Without hesitation over 300 of those present surged forward, hungry for more of God. As he and the pastors prayed, the Holy Spirit descended. The revelation of the Father's heart of love had come to Christian Life Centre Mount Annan. The next day the Sunday morning service started at 9:30 A.M. and concluded at 2:30 P.M. The Holy Spirit came again and again in every service that followed.

## Where Is the Cloud?

During this series of meetings, the assistant superintendent of the Assemblies of God in Australia rang and asked me to consider going to Toronto. I immediately felt positive about this because I recognized that this was the same Holy Spirit power that had changed my own life so dramatically 30 years before.

When the itinerant evangelist suggested to the congregation that Kathy and I go to Toronto to get some deeper understanding of what had just happened, the congregation responded with an abundant love offering. At the service that night was a pastor friend who was feeling very discouraged in his ministry. We decided to give him $1,000 of that offering to help him go to Toronto as well. The pledge needed to come in by the next Sunday, as we had booked our airline tickets by faith for the following day. As we have witnessed so many times since, God responded to our faith by not only providing the amount pledged, the extra $1,000 and more, but also an increase in tithes and offerings that Sunday! We realized this was a God thing and we were really meant to go to Toronto.

The first meeting we attended was the last meeting in the old building of the Airport church at the end of the runway. We didn't know what was going to happen or what God had in store. We spent our first day visiting Niagara Falls. On our way back we decided to find the building while it was still daylight so that we would have no difficulty that night. It was 4.30 P.M., and to our amazement there was already a lineup of people waiting for the 7:30 P.M. meeting to start! We decided it would be prudent to join the line straightaway. If this was God, we had no intention of missing anything. So we waited in the freezing cold for three hours, talking to fellow pilgrims from all over the world.

We happened upon the preservice prayer meeting and were astounded at the noises and manifestations taking place in that room. It was a great meeting that night, nothing spectacular; but when Jeremy Sinnott invited the Holy Spirit to come as we all lined up across the room, suddenly there came wave upon wave of the Spirit's power. Kathy and I lay on the floor for a couple of hours in the presence of the Lord, impacted in a way like never before. So began a life-changing week for us. We were part of a group of 35 Australians so hungry for more. Every meeting we would rush to the front rows, disregarding any signs on the seats. If they were taken, we simply got some chairs from the back of the auditorium and made a new front row with them. The team at Toronto was so gracious to us as they made room for our hunger to be satisfied.

We were so impacted by our week in Toronto that upon our return, we prayed with our leadership team and committed the church to revival—hence the church's logo and motto "A church committed to revival." We found it an incredible thing how this anointing was so transferable and transportable. Two days after we returned from Toronto, I flew to the northeast of Thailand. To our amazement the Holy Spirit fell again—upon village people who had no knowledge of what God was doing and had never experienced His power before or even seen anyone fall to the floor. The same anointing was present.

From that very first weekend, the Holy Spirit never failed to show up at any meeting. Ninety-five percent of our people immediately embraced what God was doing. We began to hold meetings throughout the week, and people came from everywhere. They came from all denominations and persuasions, clergy and lay people alike, all hungry for more of God.

Many people, after spending hours on the floor in the presence of God, reported amazing testimonies of healing, restoration and life-changing transformations. There was a young woman whose natural father had died while she was still in her mother's womb. Although she grew up with a stepfather, from time to time she noticed there was an inexplicable gap and a deep, gnawing emptiness inside. However, she would think to herself, *Well, that's life: you just have to get on with it.* There was something else though that caused her much pain. She had noticed that whenever any male other than her husband would hug her in welcome or friendship, she would recoil on the inside. She had begun to think that maybe she had been abused when she was young, although she had no memory of such an event. She had been calling out to God to help her.

The next day when she came for prayer for more at the end of the service, she had no idea what was about to happen. As my wife stepped forward to pray for this young woman and before she could even lay hands on her, Kathy grabbed her own stomach and cried out, "Oh, the pain!" With that, the young woman fell to the floor, curled up in the fetal position, sobbing, and cried out in a loud voice, "Daddy. I want my daddy."

After two and a half hours of Holy Ghost ministry, she reported that Jesus had come and put His arms around her and said, "I'll be your daddy." She had been healed of that aching emptiness. That night after one of the men of the church embraced her with a welcoming hug, she testified that for the first time for as long as she could remember, she did not recoil on the inside but felt and received the Father's love for her. Today, the young woman retains a passionate and intense love for God, a deep compassion for others and literally still shines with His glory and anointing.

We commenced a building extension to accommodate the increase God had given us. Our architect and builder were invited to come to the service, so we could pray for them and their wives before construction began. They all fell to the floor and remained that way on the stage till the end of the meeting. When they got to their feet at the end of the service, the builder's wife testified that she had been healed of a back condition she had suffered for 16 years. What astounded her was that there was no way she could have laid straight on her back on a hard floor like that before. God had worked an amazing miracle of healing that we hadn't even asked for.

Our church has continued to hold a minimum of five services per week since November 1994. Every meeting has been honored by the presence of the Holy Spirit—sometimes with power, sometimes with His sweet fragrance, sometimes in high worship and sometimes with a holy hush where no one dares move or speak. There has been no abating but, rather, an increasing intensity of the power and presence of God.

Visitors of all persuasions, have often commented that God is in this church. Many of our guest speakers instantly recognize that Mount Annan is a place without walls and fences and with no barriers to the move of the Holy Spirit.

## Walking in God's Love and Giving It Away

In February 1995, Val and Brenda Dodd from Toronto Airport Christian Fellowship were guest speakers at our first renewal/revival conference attended by leaders and people from all over the nation. They laid down some essentials about maintaining and pastoring a move of God. Two key principles we quickly embraced at Mount Annan were (1) not putting anyone's name on it—"This will be for the LORD's renown for an everlasting sign, which will not be destroyed" (Isa. 55:13, *NIV*); and (2) walking in God's love and giving it away—"A generous man will prosper; he who refreshes others will himself be refreshed" (Prov. 11:25, *NIV*).

We have been very careful not to claim any of the credit for what the Lord has done and yet, at the same time, we are humbled by the way the Lord has lifted the profile of the church. We recognize the privilege and are determined to carefully guard, guide and carry the presence of the Lord. It is all about Him—His name, His renown, His glory and His kingdom.

One key to maintaining the move of the Holy Spirit in our local church has been the desire and practice to give it away to the body of Christ locally, nationally and internationally. Mount Annan, recognized as a well for revival, holds major conferences, mini-conferences, training and equipping days and sends out speakers and teams to the nations.

Pastors from many other denominations entrust their people to come to Mount Annan to receive what God has for them. There is no doubt in their minds that the people God has given them to shepherd will return to the house from which they were sent. They come from everywhere, sometimes driving more than two hours in each direction to attend. The things they have in common are a passion for God, a desire to worship Him and a hunger for more.

# another 1,000 cubits

As a visionary leader I am committed to the move of the Spirit and to revival. We turned our heads toward it, entered the river and, in faith, continue to move further on and out. We will pursue this until we hear differently from God. The future is full of challenge and blessing as the church seeks to fulfil its destiny in God.

With a local, national and international calling for revival, the church is being mobilized in every area.

We cannot do this by ourselves. My belief for the future involves high levels of resources and networking with other leading revival churches and ministries. We have come too far to turn back and, like the disciples of old, we say, Where else can we go? (See John 6:68.) Our desire and vision for our church and leadership team is that God will take each of us to a place in Him where we have no option but to be a credible and incredible witness.

# experiencing God's rest

## BILL SUBRITZKY

*Bill Subritzky, formerly an influential attorney and business-man in Auckland, New Zealand, has for nearly 30 years trav-eled all over the world with a powerful ministry of evangelism, healing and deliverance. He has written 11 books, some of which have been translated into many languages, and has spoken at seven world conventions of the Full Gospel Businessmen's Fellowship. Carol and I first met Bill in England when we attended conferences he was holding there. Imagine our surprise when we saw him sitting in a meeting we were leading at Max Legg's church in Auckland! Bill was powerfully touched by the Holy Spirit that night and was forever changed. —J. A.*

In 24 years of ministry I have been privileged to conduct cru-sades on most continents, including Africa, South America, North America, Europe and around the Pacific basin. It has been my privilege to see tens of thousands of people fall under the power of the Holy Spirit in these crusades.

I can recall particularly dramatic experiences in Papua New Guinea and in some of the Pacific Islands where hundreds fell simultaneously and lay for hours under the power of the Spirit. I have also prayed for people individually for this experience. In all these years, however, and despite the fact that people have prayed for me, I have never fallen under the power of the Holy Spirit.

For the 12 months prior to the visit of John and Carol Arnott to New Zealand, I had received many letters and faxes from around the world, asking for my view on the Toronto

Blessing. But I refused to make any comment until I had personally observed what was happening.

The visit of Rodney Howard-Browne to New Zealand in April of that year satisfied me that this was truly a move of God. Although I had watched several videos that presented arguments against this particular move of the Spirit, I went to Rodney's seminars with an open mind. I sat in them for 10 hours. As I carefully watched, I sensed the anointing of the Holy Spirit falling in the meetings. I watched people fall around me, laughing, and I knew that the anointing of God was present.

When some weeks later I learned that John and Carol Arnott were due to visit New Zealand, I was anxious to be present in their meetings. I went with a completely open mind and told the Lord I would receive anything He had for me.

On the morning of the first session at the Arnotts' meetings, I sensed the power of God as John spoke in his very calm yet anointed way. At the conclusion of the meeting, they moved around in order to pray for people.

One of the nights that I attended the meetings, I was seated in the center aisle near the back of the hall. There were over 2,000 people present and I wondered whether the Arnotts would ever reach me.

John asked that every second row be vacated so that he and Carol could move through the rows as they prayed for people. I watched as the various rows emptied and found that I was sitting in a row that would remain. My wife, Pat, was with me.

As Carol Arnott approached me and laid hands upon me, she recognized me. I had previously been with them in meetings in both Hungary and Brighton, although, quite frankly, I had forgotten that fact. Carol began to pray with me and I sensed the power of God falling on me in a mighty way. The next thing I knew I was slumped between the seats, slain in the Spirit. I must have been there for nearly two hours. During this whole period, both Carol and others were praying with me.

Toward the end of this time, I suddenly felt a surge of joy in my heart and a desire to laugh. This joy flowed up from my belly and into my mouth, and I began laughing heartily. I went on and on for probably 30 minutes. I knew the real joy and peace of the Lord.

The next morning, I was asked to testify on the public platform. I was able to get out part of my testimony before the power of God fell on me again and I spent the next two hours on the platform while the meeting continued. Carol also came and prayed for me and was slain in the Spirit herself.

That night I was asked to testify again, but I had only said a few words before the power of God fell on me. The Lord gave me the words, "And they say this is not of Me." I barely uttered them before deep laughter came from within me, and again I was slain in the Spirit and spent the next two hours on the platform in the company of many others who were similarly slain in the Spirit. During the course of the meetings, I watched as various people attempted to testify, but the mighty power of God fell upon them.

The effect of this experience on me has been dramatic. While I was on the floor, the Lord said to me very clearly, "You have given out for years; now I am giving in to You." In other words, He was filling me afresh with His Spirit. Over the years, as an evangelist, I have prayed for tens of thousands of people in all sorts of situations, and it has been a very wearying experience. But now the Scripture in Acts 3:19 that talks of times of refreshing from the presence of the Lord has become a tremendous reality for me. So, too, have the words of Hebrews 4:9,10: "There remains therefore a Sabbath rest for the people of God. For the one who has entered His rest has himself also rested from his works." I could never understand that Scripture fully; but now I sense that I have entered God's rest. The peace of God has filled me completely.

As I have conducted further crusades in Papua New Guinea, I have ceased to work in the flesh and have relied totally upon the Holy Spirit. Whereas in the past I was worn out after three nights of crusades, I have been able to conduct four major crusades with tens of thousands of people present, as well as lead several major seminars. I am much more relaxed in the Spirit and I can hear the voice of the Lord much more clearly. The anointing of my ministry has increased dramatically.

The other major manifestation within me has been something I never anticipated. I have always believed that men should not cry. However, since I have had this experience of the Spirit, I have found that quite frequently, as the power of the Holy Spirit has come upon me, I have wanted to weep. I know that a great cleansing has been taking place within me and a sense of God's peace and joy has filled me in a way I have never known before. I also have a greater thirst for God. The reality of His presence is quite overwhelming.

When I was born again, a great vividness of color came into my life. I had never seen the grass so green, the trees so beautiful or heard the birds sing so sweetly. I felt exactly the same way the morning after I received this Holy Spirit refreshing. It was just as though I had been born again. As I looked around me, I could not get over the vividness of color. Everything seemed to take on new life.

Since that day, the Word of God has become even more vital and real to me. As I read the Word, I feel that I am being bathed and refreshed in it. I have a greater thirst for God and know His peace in a special way. I also sense a new vitality and freshness in my preaching. My evangelistic messages have taken on a new dimension. I am seeing many more people respond as the Holy Spirit moves. The gift of faith seems to have taken on a new dimension for me and I have been privileged to see many people mightily touched under the anointing of the Holy Spirit as I have prayed for them.

The effect upon my adult children has also been dramatic. Three of our four children, with their spouses, were present in the meetings. In the case of my daughter, Maria, and my two daughters-in-law, God has dealt with some of their deep hurts from long ago. Ever since the meetings were held, there has been a deep transforming work taking place within them. All of my family say they sense a deeper love for one another in their marriages and also for the Lord. For myself, I believe I have become a more gentle person.

I thank God for this wonderful move of the Spirit and for the loyal witness of John and Carol Arnott and their team.

# pilgrim's progress: reflections on a journey

## MARGARET M. POLOMA

---

*Dr. Margaret Poloma is professor emeritus of sociology at the University of Akron, Ohio, and visiting professor of graduate religion and sociology at Vanguard University of Southern California. She has been doing research on Pentecostal-Charismatic Christianity for over 20 years and has written extensively on the topic. Early in 1995, Margaret approached me and asked about doing a survey of a test group of people who had been to Toronto. She was curious about the impact and long-term fruit of their experience. That survey and a follow-up study she did two years later were amazing and very helpful. In this chapter Margaret helps us take a couple of steps back to consider the bigger picture of the role of the Father's Blessing in a Christian's spiritual journey. —J. A.*

*Remain in me, and I will remain in you. No branch can bear fruit by itself; it must remain in the vine. Neither can you bear fruit unless you remain in me (John 15:4, NIV).*

When John Arnott asked me to write an article about how God has touched my life through the renewal at the Toronto Airport Christian Fellowship, I was somewhat ambivalent. During the years I had been doing research on the renewal, I marveled over the many good things bestowed through the Toronto Blessing. The sociological surveys I conducted in 1995 and again in 1997 demonstrate beyond a doubt that countless people have been refreshed by the river of mercy that flowed through TACF, tributaries of which can be found not only throughout North America but also around the world.[1]

Although I was blessed to hear the other accounts of people being blessed, there were times that I felt like a little girl looking through a glass pane watching a wonderful party. Even though the love of God often stirred me to sing, laugh, dance, weep in His presence, feel surges of power as I prayed for others, and fall to the floor (carpet time), paradoxically there was also a sense of being a stranger to it all. As a sociologist, I knew how to play and to enjoy the role of a voyeur, but there were times I felt I was still missing the party. I had no personal story to tell—at least not one that could compare with the many dramatic accounts I had heard from the lips of others.

As I examined my experiences within the context of my 20-plus years of involvement with charismatic Christianity, I recognized that Toronto had not changed my life as decidedly as my conversion experience of Spirit baptism and the many years of spiritual direction received from those within the Catholic Christian community. This feeling of being a stranger—simultaneously both inside and outside the Toronto Blessing—led me to prayer as I sought guidance for this article. The word I heard within me was "Margaret, this isn't to be an article about you. It is to be about the larger Christian community and how the renewal fits into ongoing pilgrimage."

Mine is the story of a pilgrim in progress, not one who has arrived at her destination. My prayer is that this personal odyssey may offer a particular word of hope to those who once swam in the river but are now toiling in the fields. I pray it may also help those who have never experienced this renewal, those who were actively involved but who are now involved in other ministries, and those who have been called to tend the glowing coals and fan the flames that continue to rise.

# a paradigm for a spiritual journey

During the early 1980s, the Catholic charismatic renewal movement (during which, it is estimated, tens of thousands of Roman Catholics experienced Spirit baptism) reached a plateau. Seeking to understand what was happening with the thousands who were touched by the Holy Spirit but then seemingly dropped out of the movement, Catholic priest Robert A. Wild wrote a book in 1984 entitled *The Post-Charismatic Experience: The New Wave of the Spirit*. His book had little or no effect on me when I first read it. Yet as I looked through the book years after, while reflecting on my Toronto experience, I found Father Wild's thesis unusually insightful. Here was a paradigm that could help me both to better understand my own spirituality and to sociologically analyze what had been happening in the current renewal.

Wild's thesis centered around three interrelated themes that great spiritual masters have identified as stages of Christian spirituality. No two journeys are ever identical; but each of the stages of the typology (first identified by the early Church fathers) seems to be present, in varying frequencies and intensities, in all personal pilgrimages. I would like to briefly describe each of the stages and then illustrate how they are reflected in the ongoing renewal at Toronto that has spread around the globe.

## Stage One: Illumination

Our discussion of spiritual pilgrimage will begin with the illuminative stage, one that is characterized by a notable revelation of

God. The illuminative stage often has been described as involving light or purification. Moses encountered God in the burning bush. Isaiah saw a vision of God "seated on a throne, high and exalted" (Isa. 6:1, *NIV*). Paul experienced a sudden "light from heaven [that] flashed around him" (Acts 9:3, *NIV*) and he heard a voice. John on the Isle of Patmos "was in the Spirit" when he heard "a loud voice like a trumpet" (Rev. 1:10, *NIV*).

If the Toronto Blessing has a predominant character, it is that of being a source of illumination about the love of God. The overwhelming majority of those who responded to my surveys (9 out of 10 persons) claimed to have come to know the Father's love in a new way and to be more in love with Jesus than ever before. My own experiences in this renewal have also centered around the invitation to experience more deeply the love that God has for me.

My pilgrimage to Toronto began in November 1994, during a therapy session! My counselor asked me a question that took me aback: "Can you say without any reservation that you love yourself?" I balked at the question. Loving oneself seemed narcissistic and not something I wished to cultivate. The counselor was a secular professional who was not prone to religious talk, but she posed a surprising challenge when I asked her to clarify. "You seem to be a person of prayer. Take your question to prayer; you will come up with something."

I did take my objections to the Lord. People were sick and homeless, dying prematurely of famine, and suffering the effects of brutal wars! In the midst of human suffering and misery, how could I focus on my inability to love myself? A gentle sense that I have come to recognize as the voice of God seemed to say, "Because you don't do such a good job of loving others either." After God had my attention, there was a pause—followed by, "You have difficulty loving others because you are so hard on yourself." Still another pause. "And you are so hard on yourself because you don't have a clue about how much I love you." Then silence. That was Wednesday morning.

On Saturday night I decided to attend an evening liturgy at St. Luke's, a charismatic Episcopal church. The two priests conducting the service had just returned from the first Catch the Fire conference in Toronto. In response to the message they heard, they put aside the designated readings for the week and focused on Ephesians 3:14-19 *(NIV):*

> For this reason I kneel before the Father, from whom his whole family in heaven and on earth derives its name. I pray that out of his glorious riches he . . . may dwell in your hearts through faith. And I pray that you, being rooted and established in love, may have power, together with all the saints, to grasp how wide and long and high and deep is the love of Christ, and to know this love that surpasses knowledge—that you may be filled to the measure of all the fullness of God.

The priests stopped after each of three readings of this passage to emphasize that this message of knowing God's love was the message of Toronto. As the service continued with a heightened emphasis on Paul's prayer, I knew that I was being called to visit Toronto. The following week found me driving to the small church in a strip mall, where I stood in line for hours, talking with other pilgrims before being admitted into the service. Once the worship time began, joy filled my spirit as I experienced in this corporate setting an intense presence of God. In the midst of the strange laughter, physical manifestations and seeming frivolity, God's presence was awesome. I found myself refreshed by the playfulness of the Spirit moving within and among those gathered.

The illuminative stage is perhaps the dominant motif of the Spirit movement, which includes historic Pentecostals, Charismatics and Third-Wavers, who believe the gifts of the Spirit are for today. Worship among Spirit-filled Christians is exuberant, often providing a sense of exhilaration and unity collectively experienced by all gathered. When words were used to describe what was happening at TACF, the message quickly became one of knowing the Father's love—a Father who delighted in playing with His children. The Toronto Blessing became the Father's Blessing, as testimony after testimony illustrated the bountiful love of God being offered both to individuals and to the gathered community.

## Stage Two: Purgation

Illumination, however, is not the end of the pilgrim's path. What it offers is an awakening experience which calls the pilgrim to abide more fully in Jesus the Vine and to be subject to pruning by the Vinedresser. Illumination inevitably gives way to purgation. Neither purgation nor illumination, however, is the final goal of a spiritual journey. The outcome, according to the spiritual masters, is a greater union of the soul with its Divine Lover; in renewal metaphor, the marriage of the bride (the soul) to the Bridegroom (Jesus). Spirit-filled Christians have not always recognized the important role purgation plays in this spiritual journey, as they often neglect to dwell on the pain of Calvary in favor of the triumphant joy of Easter. They can tend to focus on the fruit of abiding in the Vine, giving little attention to the ongoing pruning process necessary for bearing fruit.

Denying the need for the purgative stage has been an ever-present temptation in renewal and revival movements where illumination is the dominant experience. Those nurtured by the spiritual exhilaration of the mountaintop are often reluctant to come down into the city. Taken with the lush green growth of intense religious experiences, many are prone to downplay, decry or even deny the reality of struggle and suffering. Like Peter, James and John on the Mount of Transfiguration, spiritual pilgrims often want to pitch their tents, proclaiming that the Kingdom has come, rather than to move on with the journey.

The temptation to pay only nodding recognition to the importance of Good Friday while focusing on the reality of Easter Sunday was one I fell into during my early involvement with the charismatic movement. It was not until I went through an extended time of purgation during a crisis in my personal life that I began to accept the reality of ongoing pruning—even for happy-clappy Christians! And when the charismatic renewal subsided, I questioned how my spirituality could ever be maintained without the dynamic Wednesday night prayer meetings. I soon found that God did not leave me, neither then nor when personal pain seemed overwhelming. I may have been in the midst of a desert experience, but God was still present. It was through this extended time of purgation that I found a new spirit of compassion for those who were suffering.

Purgation can take different metaphorical faces in the Scriptures. Jesus' teaching on the divine vinedresser reflects this stage. The beloved who wandered the streets and was beaten by the watchmen while searching for her beloved in the Song of Solomon is another picture of purgation. A more common illustration is that of the desert experience. Moses' experience of the burning bush was followed by a long desert experience during which God spoke with him under a cloud. Jesus' experience of being tempted in the desert during His long fast may be seen as purgation that followed an illuminative experience of the Father as he was baptized by John. Purgation represents a time of seeming darkness when God seems absent, especially after intense illumination.

Good Friday, although undoubtedly the most significant purgative experience of Jesus, was certainly not the only one. Some writers have seen the many years Jesus spent in Nazareth in an ordinary life that prepared him for those few short years of ministry as a period of purgation. Ordinary humdrum times when nothing of spiritual significance seems to be occurring, especially after periods of intense illumination, are also a type of purgation. The God who seemed so near, so present and so active, now seems absent.

Many pilgrims who came to Toronto reported that they had experienced a season of varying degrees and types of purgation. Of those who responded to my 1995 survey, 50 percent said that when they first visited Toronto, they were "experiencing spiritual dryness and great discouragement." Not only were they dry spiritually, but many were also carrying emotional, mental and physical burdens and were hoping for a healing touch from God. Most did find some degree of healing through the illuminative experiences of Toronto and Toronto-like renewal sites. For at least some, however, purgation continued playing as an unseen program in the background, returning to the primary screen once again after the much-needed respite. I continued to meet people who had been touched by the renewal, only to find that those still dancing at the party could not understand them when pain and suffering once again surfaced.

Lacking space for the purgative stage, the charismatic grid tends to demonize suffering, rather than see it as a necessary component of mature spirituality. Whether or not we permit dryness, pain and suffering into our paradigm, the purgative will inevitably surface for those in the Spirit movement, just as it does for those outside it. The renewal music and dancing does stop, and the soul is filled with a dark silence in which it can find a deeper unity with the One with whom it craves union.

### Stage Three: Unity and Love

The unitive stage of spirituality can be regarded as a time during which the soul learns to love in darkness. In a sense the outward signs are stilled, the sensual appetites are quieted, and the mind is at rest, creating a kind of darkness in which God alone is light. It represents a drawing into a mystical oneness with God that also releases a power to love others more deeply. While many have encountered illumination and some purgation during their involvement with renewal, still others have tasted of divine union. Perhaps the outward symbol of this experience is resting in the Spirit (or doing carpet time), a common experience during the prayer time following the formal meetings. It is well summarized by a statement from a friend concerning his first visit to TACF: "I was glued to the carpet and filled with liquid love. My life has not been the same!"

The spiritual journey is not over when the renewal music stops, the manifestations subside and the crowds disperse. On the contrary, this may be when the soul is able to enter more deeply than ever before into the love of God. Such a person may recognize that unity with God is not a mass expedition, any more than the wedding ceremony and reception represent the high point of marriage for a couple deeply in love. This does not necessarily mean that the person stops coming to renewal services—only that these exuberant services may no longer satisfy the need for a deeper union with the Bridegroom.

I can recall my own mounting discomfort with renewal services as I found them increasingly less satisfying. I cried out to God, "I know You are still working in these services, but they are making me crazy! If You want me to stay with the renewal, please give me a place where I can witness what You are doing while You can do what you need to do within me." The Lord provided such a place in what has come to be known as Shiloh Church, founded by Jeff and Beth Metzger in Canton, Ohio. In Shiloh, examples of all three of the stages can be found among the small community that gathers for Sunday morning service and the Thursday night outreach.

When I first started attending the small gatherings at Jeff and Beth's home in the summer of 1996, what I saw and experienced reminded me of early Toronto. The only props were renewal music playing in the background and the quiet offer of prayer with those who wandered in and out on Thursday nights. While there has been a rotation of people in and out of Shiloh over the years, the intense sweet presence of God has been a constant. Laughing, weeping, shaking and dancing often accompany this presence (especially for newcomers), but that is not its main drawing card. For me, Shiloh has been a place where I can encounter God in silence and solitude in the midst of the outward charismatic experiences, just as I could during the prayer time each night in Toronto. It is a place where I can be still and know that God is God.

# concluding reflections

Although I would describe renewal as primarily a time of fresh illumination—a time of encountering the burning bush through the gifts and manifestations of the Holy Spirit—pilgrims come at different stages of their own personal journeys. Some may experience a release from a desert experience, others may remain in Nazareth, some may enjoy only a brief respite from purgation, and still others may be in the "cloud of unknowing" that has been used to describe the mysterious unitive stage. Since no one on the journey has yet arrived, it is best not to judge one stage as being better than another. I have found it helpful to think of illumination and purgation in ongoing interaction to bring the soul into a deeper unity with its creator.

Over the past 20 years, God has slowly but surely moved me away from the kind of elitism that tempted me during my earlier years in the charismatic renewal movement. It is all too easy to think of illumination as being the final goal, causing the same spiritual pride to develop within us that existed in the early Christian gnostics.

While the renewal has been an instrument of God to heighten illumination, it has not done as well historically in dealing with purgation. This is true of the purgation symbolized by the wandering in the desert as well as that of the simple time of Nazareth. There is often a disparaging attitude toward those who are not "in the river," "at the party" or "flowing with the spirit," which reflects an inability of many to see the spiritual journey is a process. As a result, many continue to seek more and more illumination without ever moving into a more permanent place of divine union.

I believe that God wants to keep the renewal going in North America as He has done in other parts of the world. I pray that God may raise up many Torontos throughout Europe and North America so that those who have never experienced the illuminative love of God—especially the young—may do so. For me, Paul's prayer for the Ephesians (3:14-19) is still the central message of the Toronto Blessing. It continues to remind me of God's desire to make us one with Him as He fills us with a deeper awareness of His own love. It is through this love that we are given the power to transform the world.

However, it is wise to remember that renewal is only one thing that God is doing in His larger Church. Many who have been touched by this fresh move of the Holy Spirit in Toronto are already in a postcharismatic experience where the everyday realities of hardship prune our natures to bear more fruit in Christ. Others are floundering; they go from one place to another always in search of, always chasing, always pursuing the latest spiritual fire, wind or water and never recognize that the seed of illumination must die in order to bear more fruit. May we all acquire a deeper understanding of the rhythms of the spiritual life for a sustained involvement on our pilgrimage.

## Note

1. *The Toronto Report,* a report presenting the findings of the 1995 survey, was published in 1996 by Terra Nova Publications in Wilshire, United Kingdom. "Inspecting the Fruit of the 'Toronto Blessing': A Sociological Assessment," an article presenting a summary of both the 1995 and 1997 data, can be found on pages 43-70 in the spring 1998 issue of *Pneuma: The Journal for the Society for Pentecostal Studies.*

# an unexpected fire

## CHÉ AHN

*Dr. Ché Ahn is senior pastor of Harvest Rock Church in Pasadena, California, and founder and president of Harvest International Ministries. Carol remembers this Korean-American pastor when he attended an early Toronto conference. She was soaking him in prayer and he was shaking violently. She could tell that God would use him in a mighty way. I met Ché later when I accepted an invitation to his new church plant— Harvest Rock. I can remember saying to myself, Why am I going to this meeting? It was January 3, 1995, and I wanted to be home in Toronto and have some time with my family over the Christmas holidays. Yet I had a definite peace about it all. The meetings in the Mott Auditorium were packed and explosive as God moved in mighty power. Ché tells the story of his amazing journey into the fire of revival. —J. A.*

The year 1993 was the worst of my life. After nine years of struggling as a pastor in Southern California, I had finally called it quits. I never thought things would turn out this way.

On a night in 1982, God had given me a vision of coming to Los Angeles, with the promise that there would be a great harvest. I had come in faith and expectancy. At 28 years old, I felt ready to single-handedly bring another Azusa Street Revival to Los Angeles. For nine years I labored together with other area pastors. We did everything we could to evangelize Southern California and to see that vision fulfilled. We held early morning prayer meetings, did open-air preaching and went door-to-door witnessing. We performed street theater, went into the ghettos and held meetings with special speakers. I diligently pursued degrees all the way through the doctoral level at a respected local seminary and devoured every book about church growth I could get my hands on. It was all to no avail.

My frustration and lack of fulfillment of the ministry vision eventually turned to despair. I sought counsel and decided the best option would be to step down from my position as senior pastor. The church accepted my resignation but asked me to stay on for a one-year transition period. I found myself sinking into a deep depression, which was very unlike me. My neck was wrenched with pain and my body felt heavy and old. My family was suffering financially from the drastic salary cut that accompanied my change of status with the church. I tried to make up the difference in income by doing some itinerant work but with little success.

It was a devastating and long six months, which culminated in our having to borrow money on the equity of our home to pay our bills. I was mad at God for bringing us to California and not fulfilling the dream I knew He had supernaturally given me. What I could not know was that God was breaking me and preparing me for 1994, the year when the dream of promised revival would begin to be realized.

In January 1994, news reached us that a major visitation of the Holy Spirit was taking place in Toronto, Canada. The Holy Spirit was descending and people were having unusually strong manifestations—various physical and emotional responses that take place when an individual encounters the raw, supernatural power of God. At the same time, a similar wave of renewal was hitting a church much closer to home, the Anaheim Vineyard Christian Fellowship.

My friend and fellow minister, Lou Engle, and I were registered for the Vineyard's annual conference there. Lou was quite excited, but I was still depressed and feeling rather cynical about anything God might do for me. Yet on the very first day, we saw with our own eyes the Holy Spirit falling on people, causing them to laugh, shake and cry out. No one was even touching them! I had heard about this holy laughter and had been convinced it was the result of suggestion or mass hysteria. But now I was seeing it firsthand and I came to believe differently; then on another day of the conference, I experienced it myself. For 20 minutes I could not stop laughing! I didn't notice until later that my deep depression was gone and that I had been catapulted beyond my own human understanding into a realm of the Spirit where there was great joy and freedom. That was my initial encounter with this kind of power and fire of God.

# first visit

My first trip to Toronto was in October 1994. Excitement was in the air as thousands flew to join the Toronto Airport Christian Fellowship for the first Catch the Fire conference. I had been touched by the move of God at our local Anaheim Vineyard, but I had heard that Toronto was the new Azusa Street for this wave of the Holy Spirit.

I do not remember many of the details of my first night at the Toronto fellowship. What I do remember is that we were packed like sardines into a building way too small for the crowd, and I was uncomfortable. I don't remember who spoke that night or what was said. I do remember, however, that what happened to me during the ministry time changed my life forever.

I had come so hungry that I almost ran to the front when the call was given for those who needed ministry. My friends and I ended up on the front row waiting to be prayed for. Having been so powerfully touched by the tangible presence of God in Anaheim and knowing about the joy and manifestations spreading from Toronto, my only goal was to get blasted by the Holy Spirit. I was desperate!

A member of the ministry team came up to me and started to pray. I felt a gentle presence of the Holy Spirit and calmly fell down on the carpet. I could hear my friends Mike and David laughing as they hit the floor. Frankly, I was envious. I wanted the laughter, but I felt almost nothing. As I lay there, I asked the Lord to show me what He wanted me to receive that night.

Immediately, God began to show me bitterness in my heart toward a particular brother in the Lord. Conviction hit me so hard that I began to weep at the sinfulness of my heart. While my friends were engulfed in holy joy, I lay there sobbing and repenting.

That night, the Holy Spirit uncovered hurts I had suppressed. Instead of confronting them, I had denied they even existed; they had developed into the damaging bitter roots of which the Bible speaks in Hebrews 12:15. Yet with the loving presence of the Holy Spirit ministering to me directly that night, I could now face the pain that was otherwise too deep to acknowledge. Though the next several months of walking it through to a resolution were not easy, there was now a presence, a leading and a grace about the whole situation that I had never before experienced. Little did I know that this encounter with God would set the stage for sweeping changes in my heart, my family, my ministry and my understanding of the Lord.

## my father

While still on the floor that night, God began to reveal an entire arena of bitterness in my heart connected to the hurts I still carried from my relationship with my father. I had been anything but a model son. My years of drugs and rebellion before I met the Lord, and my father's stern discipline, had made our relationship difficult.

With tears I repented and immediately I sensed an overwhelming grace. In the months that followed, my father and I reconciled, and a spirit of rejection was broken off of me forever. The Scriptures say that God "will turn the hearts of the fathers to their children, and the hearts of the children to their fathers" before Christ comes back (Mal. 4:6, *NIV*). That is exactly what I have experienced and what is happening to many others during this current move of the Spirit.

# the ways of God

Many people have criticized this move of God as a laughing revival or just frivolous activity. They have mocked and scorned the unusual signs that accompany this visitation. Yet we will know a tree by its fruit. My observation and personal experience is that God is also doing a deep work of convicting us of our sin. He is giving us the grace to resolve root issues that have not been addressed and that would, if left to grow, defile many. To all who will cooperate with Him, He is bringing tremendous freedom, satisfaction and joy. The kingdom of God truly is "righteousness and peace and joy in the Holy Spirit" (Rom. 14:17, *NKJV*).

Countless testimonies of healing of the inner man bear witness to the fruit of this renewal. From Canada throughout the world, millions of people report changed lives after being touched by God in very personal ways. Many recount newfound feelings of acceptance through our heavenly Father's love, feelings of forgiveness toward others where there was once bitterness, and wholeness where there had been emotional devastation.

The healing with my father set the stage for an incredible healing of my marriage. As I was set free from lifelong rejection, I could now offer my wife, Sue, more love than ever before; and she was released from all the rejection I had given her. It was a much-needed wind of God in a marriage that had been struggling for years.

As I continued in the stream of love that God was issuing forth from Toronto, God lovingly revealed more sins to me and poured out His Spirit in such a way that I could overcome the very root of them. Sins that were deeply ingrained in my life have fallen off like shackles from a slave. I have never felt so free! It feels as though, even after walking with the Lord for 20 years, I am being born again and again.

I believe that in this move of God, for many believers there is more true repentance taking place than at any other time in their walk with Jesus. I know this is true in my own life. The goodness of God leads to repentance (see Rom. 2:4). Nothing changes us like the love of God! This is indeed "a more excellent way" to walk in the Lord (1 Cor. 12:31).

# the more excellent way

Not only did all the dynamics begin to change in my personal life, but I also began to see a whole new realm of God's power in ministry. God so arranged it that John Arnott came and helped us host renewal services in Pasadena. This launched a series of protracted meetings and authentic renewal for us in Southern California, and it also led to the birthing of a worldwide ministry out of our new church, Harvest Rock.

Hundreds of pastors from around the globe have come to drink from the waters now flowing in Pasadena that were launched by the river in Toronto. Many have linked arms with us to extend ministry to every corner of the globe. Our missions outreach has expanded to carry this renewal to remote areas in Africa, Tibet and Malaysia. Masses in India have crowded into our meetings to receive this touch of God.

Ministers who, like me, wanted to quit have been revived. Marriages that had become a shell of convenience have been transformed into ministry teams. Struggling believers who thought the best had come and gone in their years of service to the Lord have found a new beginning and an intimate and powerful relationship with God. It all has come through the tangible, loving presence of God that is the hallmark of this renewal.

Now I want to share with you two examples of how this encounter with Him changes the way we perceive ministry. Let me tell you the story of Akiko. This young Japanese woman came reluctantly to one of our renewal services. She had been invited by her friend, a Japanese seminary student. At one of our meetings just days earlier, he had experienced a powerful encounter with the Lord, had been filled with the Holy Spirit and had spoken in tongues, much to his own surprise; he had previously mocked charismatics!

I first saw Akiko after the service and remember asking her if she spoke English. "A little," she replied. I asked her if she wanted to accept Jesus into her heart. Hesitating briefly, she countered, "No, I cannot. My father is a Shinto. My mother is a Buddhist." I could understand Akiko's position. Having visited Japan, I knew that less than 1 percent of that country's population are Christians. A Japanese must readily conform to the norm of his society. Becoming a Christian is too contrary to the norm and means, in essence, renouncing the family and cultural heritage.

I then asked if I could pray just a blessing upon her anyway and she said yes. I simply asked the Holy Spirit to give a revelation of Jesus to Akiko (see Eph. 1:17). As soon as the words left my mouth, the Holy Spirit fell on her. She slumped to the floor and remained there 20 minutes under a wonderfully heavy presence of God! I thought it was fascinating that God would touch a nonbeliever in such a way.

After she had lain on the floor for some time, I knelt down and asked if Jesus had revealed Himself to her. She nodded her head up and down. I asked once more if she would like to invite Jesus into her heart and become a follower of Him, and she nodded yes! Together we prayed the sinner's prayer. God rested His presence on this young woman, and Akiko has continued walking as a beautiful, committed Christian.

I could have shared with her my best apologetics about how Jesus is superior to Buddha; I could have spoken with great fervor and insight. I could have talked to Akiko until I was blue in the face, but most likely it would not have changed her mind about Jesus. Yet when Akiko experienced firsthand the love, presence and power of the Holy Spirit, her heart was opened and she received the new birth! There is no substitute for an encounter with God, whether you are a believer or not! Akiko's experience that night changed my whole philosophy of evangelism: share the matchless reality of the Holy Spirit first and the fruit will be incredible!

# healings

Another mark of this river of renewal is the miraculous presence of the Holy Spirit to bring healing to people. One night during our ministry time, a Korean student was lying on the floor. I had been asked to come and pray for her because some people thought her shaking and speaking in tongues was odd and perhaps demonic. When I came to her, I immediately reassured her friends that the Holy Spirit was strong upon her, and they should not be concerned. This was the sovereign work of God and not the devil.

A few weeks later her pastor told me what happened to her. He had come with his whole congregation that night to receive from the Lord. He had helped pray for and had witnessed what happened to this young woman. He explained that she had severe scoliosis and was, in fact, scheduled to have surgery. While she was on the floor receiving the Holy Spirit's ministry, God gave her a new prayer language and healed her back. When the doctors took X rays the following week, they were dumbfounded. Her back was straight! This is only one of the many incredible miracles we have seen during this outpouring.

## the bottom line of renewal

The bottom line is that the work of God must be done by God, not by our human efforts or programs. God chose a humble man and his wife in Toronto, a man who would take his hands off and allow God to demonstrate His love and healing in the ways He saw fit. From Canada the river spread to the world, bringing salvation, renewal, refreshing, repentance, healing and deliverance. Relationships were healed and changed. Churches were given fresh fire for the things of God and began to impact their communities. A foundation for revival, where entire cities get turned upside down, continues to be laid by Christians who are personally empowered by their loving Lord.

The fact is that one touch of God's love can accomplish more in a minute than our best-planned efforts can accomplish in a lifetime. One intimate relationship *with* God can influence more people for Him than any top theologian's discussion *about* God. One humbling minute of experiencing God's power on you, in you and through you will forever change your concept and manner of ministry. You will willingly and gratefully back away from your own agenda and simply become an instrument in the Master's hands. You will only want to do His bidding.

God will get all the glory and you will fall wonderfully more in love with Him every day. You will require Him as your urgent need, your most gracious love and your very life's breath. You will serve Him with joy and see His success upon you. His holiness will become attainable in your life because of His love.

You will be forever changed and so will those around you. You will find this tangible presence of God wonderfully transferable to all for whom you pray. You will begin to hunger and search for more of Him and continually be filled by His presence. This will become your lifestyle. You will find Him true and faithful to all He says He is, and He alone will have your heart. You will sense His pleasure in you in a whole new way. That is what the Toronto renewal is all about: a wonderfully unexpected fire with life-giving love and eternal power.

# God with us

JOHN ARNOTT

---

We had no idea in those early days that seven years later our church in Toronto would still be holding nightly revival meetings! We could not have known that over 3 million would attend our services and conferences and be powerfully blessed by the Spirit of God, and that thousands would commit their lives to Christ. We were overwhelmingly surprised when many Christian leaders from around the world came thirsting for a more intimate relationship with God. For our part, we have only tried to stay simple and humble and keep out of the Holy Spirit's way, as even now He continues to move in power upon the hungry.

Our hearts have been thrilled by so many miraculous testimonies. We have watched in amazement as this fire of God has become a worldwide phenomenon, touching virtually every nation as it has spread from one country to another. You cannot imagine the gratitude Carol and I have to the Holy Spirit who has used us, our church and our ministry team.

It has been our privilege to travel to more than 30 countries around the world to share the good news that revival has come. It is here now; you don't have to wait. God is visiting Earth. We have Emmanuel—God is with us! He is not the great I was, or the great I will be, but the Great I AM, the ever-present One who is with us right now and not just in a theological sense. His presence is so real that you can feel and experience it. Jesus earnestly prayed "that the love with which You loved Me may be in them, and I in them" (John 17:26, *NKJV*). He has come to bind up the brokenhearted, heal the bruised, set the captives free and declare good news to the poor (see Isa. 61:1-3).

I hope your faith has been strengthened by these testimonies of the mighty impact of the Holy Spirit on people's lives. They came to Toronto or to one of our international meetings and were truly touched by God. I hope we have resolved some of your fears that may have been unfairly stirred up by critics or by wrong theology. I pray that you have not missed out on the greatest blessing of your Christian life because of misinformation or slanted reporting. With the testimony of two or three witnesses may every word be established (see 2 Cor. 13:1). May their stories spur you on to seek more of God's infilling love and power. May your hunger for Him overtake your fears.

Some in this book, like Jack Taylor and Joseph Garlington, were familiar names to the Body of Christ before they came to Toronto. Others were relatively unknown, yet God placed in them a deposit of love, faith and trust that has since launched them into powerful and significant ministries. One thing is certain: The Church today is not the same as it was seven years ago. There is now a growing expectation worldwide that when believers meet together and ask God to come with His manifest presence, something is supposed to happen! We have seen miracles, conversions, healings, signs, wonders and, perhaps the greatest sign of all, a deep and profound love for Christ that goes beyond anything we have ever experienced. Jesus commanded us in Matthew 22:37 to love the Lord with all our hearts, souls and minds. When we are filled with a fresh love for Him, there is a growing desire to love and serve one another with our various ministries of healing, help and salvation. We who have, in the past, been so overly busy working for God, feel like we have returned to our first love (see Rev. 2:4), thanks to the Holy Spirit's refreshing.

What we are attempting to communicate to you is simply this: God is not only real, but He is also available to you! He wants to fill your life with an abundance of love, joy and peace. If you have never received Christ as your personal Savior, let me urge you to do so right now, in the privacy of this moment. Just get honest with yourself and with God for a minute. Admit that you are a sinner and that you need His help. The truth is clearly stated in God's Word: "For God so loved the world, that He gave His only begotten Son, that whoever believes in Him should not perish, but have everlasting life" (John 3:16). Believe in Him for yourself, right now. Act on the simplicity of the verse I have just quoted; there is nothing for you to do in a religious sense. Only believe that everything a righteous God would require of you has already been completed by Jesus Christ when He died on the cross for you—when He traded His perfect life for yours.

Pray this little prayer with me now:

*Dear God, I come humbly to You. I believe that Jesus Christ died on the cross for me. I open my heart to You, Lord. Come into my life. Wash me clean from all my sins and give me the gift of salvation. I receive forgiveness in childlike faith. I take You now as my very own personal Savior. Thank You, Lord, for forgiving me and bringing the good news of Jesus Christ to me. I receive Your free gift of eternal life. From this moment on You are my Savior. I am a Christian, and You are the Lord of my life. Amen.*

If you want to know more about who Jesus is, I suggest that you read the book of John from the New Testament in the Bible. It tells the story of how God sent His sinless Son to be sin for us so that we can become the righteousness of God in Him (see 2 Cor. 5:21). This wonderful news is your opportunity to go from nothing to everything! Jesus is truly Jehovah, the Lord who saves.

For those of you who are hungry for more of God's personal touch in your lives, please know that it is the Holy Spirit you need and that He is yours for the asking. Jesus said in John 7:37-39 (*NKJV*): "If anyone thirsts, let him come to Me and drink. He who believes in Me, as the Scripture has said, out of his [innermost being] will flow rivers of living water. But this He spoke concerning the Spirit, whom those believing in Him would receive."

In the testimonies you have just read, well-known leaders in the Body of Christ have honestly shared how they were hungry and thirsty for a deeper encounter with God. When they humbled themselves and asked Jesus for more, they were not disappointed. Why don't you do the same? Why don't you do it right now? Go before the Lord in humility. Ask Him to fill you afresh with His Holy Spirit. It is your Father's promise. Listen to what Jesus said: "Wait for the gift my Father promised, which you have heard me speak about. For John baptized with water, but in a few days you will be baptized with the Holy Spirit" (Acts 1:4,5, *NIV*). To be baptized means to be immersed, surrounded by the Holy Spirit's power and presence, inside and out. This baptism was the secret of the Early Church in winning their pagan world to Christ and in loving Jesus more than their own lives.

Know too that this is not a one-time experience; it is to be renewed daily. Ephesians 5:18 commands us to "be filled with the Spirit." The original text implies that we should *keep on being refilled* with the Spirit. The apostles were filled in Acts 2:4, yet in Acts 4:31 they were all filled again. Some of us are long overdue to be filled afresh with the Holy Spirit.

Pray with me right now, won't you?

*Lord Jesus, I come to You in humility and simplicity of heart. I ask You to forgive my complacency and give me a hunger for*

*Your presence. I want my first love again. I want to be closer to You. Give me more of Your Holy Spirit's power in my life. Fill me, Lord. Baptize me, Father, according to Your promise. I want to be more effective for You. I want to be more like You. I want to be filled with You—filled with all the fullness of God. In Jesus' name I pray, amen.*

May God bless you and fill you as you seek His loving face.

# ministry contact

Toronto Airport Christian Fellowship (TACF) is a local, cell-based church and international ministry center located in Toronto, Ontario, Canada. It is the founding member of the Partners in Harvest church network. Since the Holy Spirit began to move in January 1994, over 2.5 million visitors from around the world have attended services at TACF. Thousands have made commitments to Christ, thousands of pastors and leaders have been refreshed and countless others have had their passion for Jesus renewed. The church supports a variety of ministries:

- *Spread the Fire* magazine, published bimonthly and mailed free to over 50,000 people
- *Catch the Fire,* a television program that broadcast across Canada and in several nations around the world
- Missions Outreach
- School of Ministry
- Bible Institute
- Children's Ministry
- Youth Ministry
- Encounter Weekends
- Prayer Ministry
- Men's and Women's Ministries
- Leadership Training
- Worship Training
- Revival Services
- Healing and Equipping Conferences

For a schedule of events and services, contact the church office or visit our website.

## TORONTO AIRPORT CHRISTIAN FELLOWSHIP
272 Attwell Drive
Toronto, Ontario
M9W 6M3

Phone:  416-674-8463
Fax: 416-674-8465
E-mail: www.info@tacf.org
Website:  www.tacf.org